PRISM

READING AND WRITING
TEACHER'S MANUAL

1

Richard O'Neill
Michele Lewis

with
Wendy Asplin
Carolyn Flores
Jeanne Lambert

CAMBRIDGE
UNIVERSITY PRESS

CAMBRIDGE
UNIVERSITY PRESS

University Printing House, Cambridge CB2 8BS, United Kingdom

One Liberty Plaza, 20th Floor, New York, NY 10006, USA

477 Williamstown Road, Port Melbourne, VIC 3207, Australia

4843/24, 2nd Floor, Ansari Road, Daryaganj, Delhi – 110002, India

79 Anson Road, #06–04/06, Singapore 079906

Cambridge University Press is part of the University of Cambridge.

It furthers the University's mission by disseminating knowledge in the pursuit of education, learning and research at the highest international levels of excellence.

www.cambridge.org
Information on this title: www.cambridge.org/9781316625088

© Cambridge University Press 2017

First published 2017

20 19 18 17 16 15 14 13 12 11 10 9 8 7 6 5 4 3 2 1

Printed in Malaysia by Vivar Printing

A catalogue record for this publication is available from the British Library

ISBN 978-1-316-62508-8 Teacher's Manual 1 Reading and Writing
ISBN 978-1-316-62427-2 Student's Book with Online Workbook 1 Reading and Writing

CONTENTS

SCOPE AND SEQUENCE

UNIT	WATCH AND LISTEN	READINGS	READING SKILLS	LANGUAGE DEVELOPMENT	
1 PLACES _Academic Disciplines_ Sociology / Urban Planning	The Top U.S. City	1: Rise of the Megacities (article) 2: Homestay Vacations: A Home away from Home (article)	_Key Skill_ Scanning for numbers _Additional Skills_ Understanding key vocabulary Using your knowledge Reading for main ideas Reading for details Scanning to find information Scanning to predict content Working out meaning Making inferences Synthesizing	Nouns, verbs, and adjectives	
2 FESTIVALS AND CELEBRATIONS _Academic Disciplines_ Anthropology / Cultural Studies	The Meaning of Independence Day	1: Celebrate! (article) 2: Muscat Festival (article)	_Key Skill_ Previewing a text _Additional Skills_ Understanding key vocabulary Scanning to predict content Reading for main ideas Reading for details Recognizing text type Synthesizing	Prepositions of time and place Adverbs of frequency	
3 THE INTERNET AND TECHNOLOGY _Academic Disciplines_ Computer Science / Engineering	Predictive Advertising	1: Someone's Always Watching You Online (Web article) 2: Video Games for Kids: Win or Lose? (essay)	_Key Skills_ Reading for main ideas Making inferences _Additional Skills_ Understanding key vocabulary Using your knowledge Scanning to predict content Reading for details Recognizing text type Synthesizing	Compound nouns Giving opinions	
4 WEATHER AND CLIMATE _Academic Disciplines_ Environmental Studies / Meteorology	Tornadoes	1: Extreme Weather (profile) 2: Surviving the Sea of Sand: How to Stay Alive in the Sahara Desert (article)	_Key Skills_ Reading for details Using your knowledge to predict content _Additional Skills_ Understanding key vocabulary Reading for main ideas Recognizing text type Synthesizing	Collocations with _temperature_ Describing a graph	

CRITICAL THINKING	GRAMMAR FOR WRITING	WRITING	ON CAMPUS
Using a T-chart Analyzing positives and negatives	Simple sentences 1: • Subject + verb *There is / there are*	*Academic Writing Skill* Capital letters and punctuation *Rhetorical Mode* Descriptive *Writing Task* Describe the place where you live. Write about its positives and its negatives. (sentences)	*Life Skill* Finding a place to live
Using an idea map to organize ideas	Simple sentences 2: • Objects and extra information • Prepositional phrases	*Academic Writing Skill* Organizing sentences into a paragraph *Rhetorical Mode* Descriptive *Writing Task* Describe a festival or special event. (paragraph)	*Life Skill* Cultural exchange
Analyzing a question	Connecting ideas • *And, also,* and *too* • Compound sentences • *However*	*Academic Writing Skill* Topic sentences *Rhetorical Mode* Opinion *Writing Task* The Internet wastes our time. It does not help us do more work. Do you agree or disagree? (paragraph)	*Study Skill* The virtual classroom
Analyzing a graph	Comparative and superlative adjectives	*Academic Writing Skills* Supporting sentences Giving examples • *Like, such as,* and *for example* *Rhetorical Mode* Descriptive *Writing Task* Describe the weather in a country or region. (paragraph)	*Life Skill* Seeing a doctor

UNIT	WATCH AND LISTEN	READINGS	READING SKILLS	LANGUAGE DEVELOPMENT	
5 SPORTS AND COMPETITION *Academic Disciplines* Sports Management / Sports Science	Skiing in the French Alps	1: Five Unusual Sports (article) 2: Tough Guy: A Race to the Limit (article)	*Key Skill* Scanning to predict content *Additional Skills* Understanding key vocabulary Previewing Reading for main ideas Reading for details Recognizing text type Understanding discourse Working out meaning Synthesizing	Prepositions of movement	
6 BUSINESS *Academic Disciplines* Business / Marketing	Amazon's Fulfillment Center	1: Are You Ready for the World of Work? (survey) 2: The Story of Google (article)	*Key Skills* Working out meaning from context Annotating a text *Additional Skills* Understanding key vocabulary Scanning to predict content Reading for main ideas Reading for details Identifying audience Making inferences Synthesizing	Collocations with *business* Business vocabulary	
7 PEOPLE *Academic Disciplines* Psychology / Sociology	The 101-Year-Old Weather Volunteer	1: Incredible People: Ben Underwood (blog post) 2: Incredible People (blog posts)	*Key Skill* Making inferences *Additional Skills* Understanding key vocabulary Scanning to predict content Reading for main ideas Reading for details Working out meaning Identifying purpose Synthesizing	Noun phrases with *of* Adjectives to describe people	
8 THE UNIVERSE *Academic Disciplines* Astronomy / Engineering	Going to the International Space Station	1: The Rise of Commercial Space Travel (article) 2: Life on Other Planets (essay)	*Key Skill* Identifying the author's purpose *Additional Skills* Understanding key vocabulary Using your knowledge Scanning to predict content Reading for main ideas Reading for details Making inferences Distinguishing fact from opinion Synthesizing	Giving evidence and supporting an argument	

CRITICAL THINKING	GRAMMAR FOR WRITING	WRITING	ON CAMPUS
Analyzing a diagram	Subject and verb agreement	**_Academic Writing Skills_** Ordering events in a process Removing unrelated information **_Rhetorical Mode_** Process **_Writing Task_** Describe the Sydney Triathlon. (paragraph)	**_Communication Skill_** Virtual communication
Using a timeline to put past events in order	The simple present and the simple past Time clauses with _when_ to describe past events	**_Academic Writing Skill_** Adding details to main facts **_Rhetorical Mode_** Narrative **_Writing Task_** Write about the history of a business. (paragraph)	**_Study Skill_** Creating checklists
Using a Venn diagram	Modals of necessity	**_Academic Writing Skill_** Concluding sentences **_Rhetorical Mode_** Explanatory **_Writing Task_** Who do you think is a good role model? Write a paragraph explaining the qualities that make that person a good role model. (paragraph)	**_Communication Skill_** Expressing your opinion
Evaluating arguments	_That_ clauses in complex sentences Infinitives of purpose	**_Academic Writing Skill_** Essay organization **_Rhetorical Mode_** Opinion **_Writing Task_** Should governments spend more money on space exploration? Give reasons and examples to support your opinion. (essay)	**_Research Skill_** Using the library

INTRODUCTION

Prism **is a five-level paired skills series for beginner- to advanced-level students of North American English.** Its five Reading and Writing and five Listening and Speaking levels are designed to equip students with the language and skills to be successful both inside and outside of the college classroom.

Prism **uses a fresh approach to Critical Thinking based on a full integration of Bloom's taxonomy to help students become well-rounded critical thinkers.** The productive half of each unit begins with Critical Thinking. This section gives students the skills and tools they need to plan and prepare for success in their Speaking or Writing Task. Learners develop lower- and higher-order thinking skills, ranging from demonstrating knowledge and understanding to in-depth evaluation and analysis of content. Margin labels in the Critical Thinking sections highlight exercises that develop Bloom's concepts.

Prism **focuses on the most relevant and important language for students of academic English based on comprehensive research.** Key vocabulary is taken from the General Service List, the Academic Word List, and the Cambridge English Corpus. The grammar selected is also corpus-informed.

Prism **goes beyond language and critical thinking skills to teach students how to be successful, engaged college students both inside and outside of the classroom.** On Campus spreads at the end of each unit introduce students to communication, study, presentation, and life skills that will help them transition to life in North American community college and university programs.

Prism **combines print and digital solutions for the modern student and program.** Online workbooks give students additional graded language and skills practice. Video resources are available to students and teachers in the same platform. Presentation Plus gives teachers modern tools to enhance their students' learning environment in the classroom.

Prism **provides assessment resources for the busy teacher.** Photocopiable unit quizzes and answer keys are included in the Teacher's Manual, with downloadable PDF and Word versions available at Cambridge.org/prism and in the Resource tab of the Cambridge Learning Management System. Writing rubrics for grading Writing Tasks in the Student's Book and on the Unit Writing Quizzes are included in the Teacher's Manual.

SERIES LEVELS

Level	Description	CEFR Levels
Prism Intro	Beginner	A1
Prism 1	Low Intermediate	A2
Prism 2	Intermediate	B1
Prism 3	High Intermediate	B2
Prism 4	Advanced	C1

TEACHING SUGGESTIONS

UNIT OPENER

Each unit opens with a striking two-page photo related to the topic, a Learning Objectives box, and an Activate Your Knowledge activity.

PURPOSE
- To introduce and generate interest in the unit topic with an engaging visual
- To set the learning objectives for the unit
- To make connections between students' background knowledge and the unit topic/theme

TEACHING SUGGESTIONS
PHOTO SPREAD

Lead an open class discussion on the connection between the unit opener photo and topic. Start off with questions like:
- *What is the first thing you notice in the photographs?*
- *What do you think of when you look at the photo?*
- *How is the photo connected to the unit title?*

ACTIVATE YOUR KNOWLEDGE

After students work in pairs to discuss the questions, have volunteers share with the class answers to questions that generated the most discussion.

You can also use the exercise to practice fluency. Instruct students to answer the questions as quickly as possible without worrying about creating grammatically correct sentences. Keep time and do not allow students more than 15–60 seconds per answer, depending on level and complexity of the question. You can then focus on accuracy when volunteers share their answers with the class.

WATCH AND LISTEN

Each unit includes a short authentic video from a respected news source that is related to the unit topic, along with exercises for students to do before, during, and after watching. The video can be played in the classroom or watched outside of class by students via the Cambridge LMS.

Note: A glossary defines above-level or specialized words that appear in the video and are essential for students to understand the main ideas so that teachers do not have to spend time pre-teaching or explaining this vocabulary while viewing.

PURPOSE
- To create a varied and dynamic learning experience
- To generate further interest in and discussion of the unit topic
- To build background knowledge and ideas on the topic
- To develop and practice key skills in prediction, comprehension, and discussion
- To personalize and give opinions on a topic

TEACHING SUGGESTIONS
PREPARING TO WATCH

Have students work in pairs to complete the Activating Your Knowledge exercise. Then have volunteers share their answers. Alternatively, students can complete this section on their own, and then compare answers with their partners.

For a livelier class discussion, look at the visuals from the Predicting Content Using Visuals exercise as a class and answer the questions together.

WHILE WATCHING

Watch the video twice, once while students listen for main ideas and once while they listen for key details. After each viewing, facilitate a discussion of students' answers and clarify any confusion. If some students still have trouble with comprehension, suggest that they watch the video again at home or during a computer lab session.

DISCUSSION

Have students work in pairs or small groups to answer the discussion questions. Have students compare their answers with another pair or group. Then have volunteers share their answers with the class. If possible, expand on their answers by making connections between their answers and the video content. For example: *That's an interesting perspective. How is it similar to what the speaker in the video mentioned? How is it different?*

For writing practice, have students write responses to the questions for homework.

READING

The first half of each unit focuses on the receptive skill of reading. Each unit includes two reading passages that provide different angles, viewpoints, and/or genres related to the unit topic.

READING 1

Reading 1 includes a reading passage on an academic topic. It provides information on the unit topic, and it gives students exposure to and practice with language and reading skills while helping them begin to generate ideas for their Writing Task.

PREPARING TO READ

PURPOSE

- To prepare students to understand the content of the reading
- To introduce, review, and/or practice key pre-reading skills
- To introduce and build key academic and topical vocabulary for the reading and for the unit Writing Task

TEACHING SUGGESTIONS

Encourage students to complete the pre-reading activities in this section in pairs or groups. This will promote a high level of engagement. Once students have completed the activities, check for understanding and offer any clarification.

Encourage or assign your students to keep a vocabulary notebook for new words. This should include new key vocabulary words, parts of speech, definitions (in the students' own words), and contextual sentences. To extend the vocabulary activity in this section, ask students to find synonyms, antonyms, or related terms for the vocabulary items they just practiced. These can then be added to their vocabulary notebooks.

Key vocabulary exercises can also be assigned ahead of time so that you can focus on the reading content and skills in class.

If time permits, have students scan Reading 1 for the key vocabulary just practiced in bold and read the sentences with each term. This will provide additional pre-reading scaffolding.

WHILE READING

PURPOSE

- To introduce, review, and/or practice key academic reading skills
- To practice reading comprehension and annotation skills
- To see and understand key vocabulary in a natural academic context
- To provide information and stimulate ideas on an academic topic
- To help students become more efficient readers

TEACHING SUGGESTIONS

Have students work in pairs or small groups to complete the activities. Students should always be prepared to support their answers from the text, so encourage them to annotate the text as they complete the activities. After students complete the activities, have volunteers share their answers with the class, along with support from the text. If necessary, facilitate clarification by referring back to the text yourself. Use guided questions to help with understanding. For example: *Take a moment to review the final sentences of Paragraph 2. What words discuss a problem?*

READING BETWEEN THE LINES

PURPOSE

- To introduce, expand on, and/or practice key reading skills related to students' ability to infer meaning, text type, purpose, audience, etc.
- To introduce, review, and/or practice key critical thinking skills applied to content from the reading passage

TEACHING SUGGESTIONS

Have students complete the activities in pairs or small groups and share their answers with the class. It is particularly important for students to be able to support their answers using the text at this point. Encourage students to work out any partial or wrong answers by asking a series of clear, guided questions like: *You thought the author meant ... What about this sentence in the reading? What information does it give us? Does this sentence change your mind about your answer?*"
After checking answers, survey students on what they found most challenging in the section. Then have students read the text again for homework, making additional annotations and notes on the challenging skills and content to be shared at the beginning of the next class or in an online forum.

DISCUSSION

PURPOSE

- To give students the opportunity to discuss and offer opinions about what they read
- To think critically about the content of the reading
- To further personalize the topic and issues in Reading 1

TEACHING SUGGESTIONS

Give students three to five minutes to discuss and jot down notes for their answers before discussing them in pairs or small groups. Monitor student groups, taking notes on common mistakes. Then, survey the students on their favorite questions and have groups volunteer to share these answers. You can provide oral or written feedback on common mistakes at the end of the section.

READING 2

Reading 2 is a reading passage on the unit topic from a different angle and often in a different format than Reading 1. It gives students additional exposure to and practice with language and reading skills while helping them generate and refine ideas for their Writing Task. It generally includes rhetorical elements that serve as a structured model for the Writing Task.

PREPARING TO READ

PURPOSE

- To prepare students to understand the content of the reading
- To introduce, review, and/or practice key pre-reading skills
- To introduce and build key academic and topical vocabulary for the reading and for the unit Writing Task

TEACHING SUGGESTIONS

As with Reading 1, encourage students to complete the activities in this section in pairs or small groups to promote a high level of engagement. Circulate among students at this time, taking notes of common areas of difficulty. Once students have completed the activities, check for understanding and offer clarification, paying particular attention to any problem areas you noted.

If you wish to extend the vocabulary activity in this section, elicit other word forms of the key vocabulary. Students can add these word forms to their vocabulary notebooks.

WHILE READING

PURPOSE

- To introduce, review, and/or practice key academic reading skills
- To practice reading comprehension and annotation skills
- To see and understand key vocabulary in a natural academic context
- To provide information and stimulate ideas on an academic topic
- To help students become more efficient readers
- To model aspects or elements of the Writing Task

TEACHING SUGGESTIONS

As with Reading 1, have students work in pairs or small groups to complete the activities. Encourage them to annotate the reading so that they are prepared to support their answers from the text. Elicit answers and explanations from the class. Remember to facilitate clarification by referring back to the text yourself, using clear, guided questions to help with understanding.

Alternatively, separate the class into multiple groups, and assign a paragraph or section of the reading to each groups. (Students should skim the rest of the passage not assigned to them.) Set a time limit for reading. Then do the exercises as a class, with each group responsible for answering and explaining the items that fall within their paragraph or section of the text.

READING BETWEEN THE LINES

PURPOSE

- To introduce, expand on, and/or practice key reading skills related to students' ability to infer meaning, text type, purpose, audience, etc.
- To introduce, review, and/or practice key critical thinking skills applied to content from the reading passage

TEACHING SUGGESTIONS

For Making Inferences activities, have students work in pairs to answer the questions. Instruct pairs to make notes in the margins about the clues from the text they use to answer the questions. Then have pairs meet up with other pairs to compare their clues. Have volunteers share their clues and answers with the class.

For other activity types, such as Recognizing Text Type or Distinguishing Fact and Opinion, have students work in pairs and then share their answers with the class as before. Then promote deeper engagement with guided questions like:

- *How is an essay different from a newspaper article?"*
- *What are common features of a* [text type]?"
- *What words in the sentence tell you that you are reading an opinion and not a fact?*
- *Can you say more about what x means?*

DISCUSSION

PURPOSE

- To personalize and expand on the ideas and content of Reading 2
- To practice synthesizing the content of the unit reading passages

TEACHING SUGGESTIONS

Before students discuss the questions in this section the first time, introduce the key skill of synthesis. Start by defining synthesis (combining and analyzing ideas from multiple sources). Stress its importance in higher education: in college or graduate school, students will be asked to synthesize ideas from a wide range of sources, to think critically about them, to make connections among them, and to add their own ideas. Note: you may need to review this information periodically with your class.

Have students answer the questions in pairs or small groups, and then ask for volunteers to share their answers with the class. Facilitate the discussion, encouraging students to make connections between Reading 1 and Reading 2. If applicable, ask students to relate the content of the unit video to this section. This is also a good context in which to introduce the Writing Task at the beginning of the Critical Thinking section and to have students consider how the content of the reading passages relates to the prompt.

To extend this activity beyond discussion, write the connections students make on the board, and have students take notes. Students can then use their notes to write sentences or a paragraph(s) describing how the ideas in all the sources discussed are connected.

LANGUAGE DEVELOPMENT

Each unit includes the introduction and practice of academic language relevant to the unit topic and readings, and useful for the unit Writing Task. The focus of this section is on vocabulary and/or grammar.

PURPOSE

- To recycle and expand on vocabulary that appears in Reading 1 or Reading 2
- To focus and expand on grammar that appears in Reading 1 or Reading 2
- To expose students to additional corpus-informed, research-based language for the unit topic and level
- To practice language and structures that students can use in the Writing Task

TEACHING SUGGESTIONS

For grammar points, review the Language Box as a class and facilitate answers to any unclear sections. Alternatively, have students review it in pairs and allow time for questions. Then have students work in pairs to complete the accompanying activities. Review students' answers, allowing time for any clarification.

For vocabulary points, have students complete the exercises in pairs. Then, review answers and allow time for any clarification. To extend this activity, have students create sentences using each term and/or make a list of synonyms, antonyms, or related words and phrases for each term. Students should also add relevant language to their vocabulary notebooks. For homework, have students annotate the readings in the unit, underlining or highlighting any language covered in this section.

WRITING

The second half of each unit focuses on the productive skill of writing. It begins with the prompt for the Writing Task and systematically equips students with the grammar and skills to plan for, prepare, and execute the task successfully.

CRITICAL THINKING

PURPOSE

- To introduce the Writing Task.
- To notice and analyze features of Reading 2 related to the Writing Task
- To help generate, develop, and organize ideas for the Writing Task.
- To teach and practice the lower-order critical thinking skills of remembering, understanding, and applying knowledge through practical brainstorming and organizational activities

- To teach and practice the higher-order critical thinking skills of analyzing, evaluating, and creating in order to prepare students for success in the Writing Task and, more generally, in the college classroom

TEACHING SUGGESTIONS

Encourage students to work through this section collaboratively in pairs or small groups to promote a high level of engagement. Facilitate their learning and progress by circulating and checking in on students as they work through this section. If time permits, have groups exchange and evaluate one another's work.

Note: Students will often be directed back to this section to review, revise, and expand on their initial ideas and notes for the Writing Task.

GRAMMAR FOR WRITING

PURPOSE

- To introduce and practice grammar that is relevant to the Writing Task
- To introduce and practice grammar that often presents trouble for students at this level of academic writing

TEACHING SUGGESTIONS

Review any Skills boxes in this section as a class, allowing time to answer questions and clarify points of confusion. Then have students work on the activities in pairs or small groups, before eliciting answers as a class.

ACADEMIC WRITING SKILLS

PURPOSE

- To present and practice academic writing skills needed to be successful in college or graduate school
- To focus on specific language and skills relevant to the Writing Task

TEACHING SUGGESTIONS

Have students read any Skills boxes on their own. Check understanding by asking guided questions like:

- *What do you notice about the parallel structure examples?*
- *What are some other examples of parallel structure?*
- *How would you describe parallel structure based on the information and examples you just read?*

Provide clarification as necessary, offering and eliciting more examples. Have students find examples in the unit readings if possible.

Students can work in pairs to complete the exercises and then share their answers with the class. Alternatively, assign exercises for homework.

WRITING TASK

PURPOSE

- To work collaboratively in preparation for the Writing Task
- To revisit, revise, and expand on work done in the Critical Thinking section
- To provide an opportunity for students to synthesize the language, skills, and ideas presented and generated in the unit
- To help students plan, draft, revise, and edit their writing

TEACHING SUGGESTIONS

Depending on time and class level, students can complete the preparation activities for homework or in class. If conducted in class, have students work on their own to complete the Plan section. They can then share their plans in pairs. Give students time to revise their plans based on feedback from their partners.

Depending on time, students can write their first drafts at home or in class. Encourage students to refer to the Task Checklist before and after writing their first drafts. The checklist can also be used in a peer review of first drafts in class.

Note: At this stage, encourage students to focus on generating and organizing their ideas, and answering the prompt, rather than perfecting their grammar, which they will focus on during the Edit stage using the Language Checklist.

Even with a peer review, it is important to provide written feedback for your students, either on their first or second drafts. When doing so, look for common mistakes in student writing. Select at least one problem sentence or area from each student's draft, and conduct an edit correction exercise either as a class or in an online discussion forum. You can also select and review a well-written sentence from each draft to serve as models and to provide positive reinforcement.

ON CAMPUS

Each unit concludes with a unique spread that teaches students concepts and skills that go beyond traditional reading and writing academic skills.

PURPOSE
- To familiarize students with all aspects of the North American college experience
- To enable students to interact and participate successfully in the college classroom
- To prepare students to navigate typical North American college campus life

TEACHING SUGGESTIONS
PREPARING TO READ

Begin with an open discussion by asking students what they know about the topic. For example:
- *What is a study plan?*
- *Have you ever written an email to a teacher or professor?*
- *How do college students choose a major?*
- *What is a virtual classroom?*

You can also write the question on the board and assign as pair work, and have students share their answers with the class.

WHILE READING

Have students read the text and complete the accompanying activities. Have them read again and check their work. You can extend these activities by asking the following questions:
- *What did you find most interesting in this reading passage?*
- *What did you understand more clearly during the second reading?*
- *Who do you think wrote the text? Why?*

PRACTICE

Have students read any skills boxes silently. Give them two minutes to discuss the information with partners before they complete the exercises. Elicit from some volunteers how the exercises practice what they read in the text.

REAL-WORLD APPLICATION

Depending on time, you may want to assign the activities in this section as homework. Having students collaborate on these real-world tasks either inside or outside of the classroom simulates a common practice in college and graduate school. At the beginning of the week you can set up a schedule so that several student groups present their work during class throughout the week.

To extend this section, assign small related research projects, as applicable. For example, have students research and report on three websites with information on choosing a college major.

PRISM WRITING TASK RUBRIC

CATEGORY	CRITERIA	SCORE
Content and Development	• Writing completes the task and fully answers the prompt. • Content is meaningful and interesting. • Main points and ideas are fully developed with good support and logic.	

Organization	• Writing is well-organized and follows the conventions of academic writing:
	  • Paragraph – topic sentence, supporting details, concluding sentence
	  • Essay – introduction with thesis, body paragraphs, conclusion
	• Rhetorical mode(s) used is appropriate to the writing task.	

Coherence, Clarity, and Unity	• Sentences within a paragraph flow logically with appropriate transitions; paragraphs within an essay flow logically with appropriate transitions. • Sentences and ideas are clear and make sense to the reader. • All sentences in a paragraph relate to the topic sentence; all paragraphs in an essay relate to the thesis.	
Vocabulary	• Vocabulary, including expressions and transition language, is accurate, appropriate, and varied. • Writing shows mastery of unit key vocabulary and Language Development.	
Grammar and Writing Skills	• Grammar is accurate, appropriate, and varied. • Writing shows mastery of unit Grammar for Writing and Language Development. • Sentence types are varied and used appropriately. • Level of formality shows an understanding of audience and purpose. • Mechanics (capitalization, punctuation, indentation, and spelling) are strong. • Writing shows mastery of unit Academic Writing Skills.	

How well does the response meet the criteria?	Recommended Score
At least 90%	20
At least 75%	15
At least 60%	10
At least 50%	5
Less than 50%	0
Total Score Possible per Section	20
Total Score Possible	100

Feedback:

STUDENT'S BOOK ANSWER KEY

UNIT 1
ACTIVATE YOUR KNOWLEDGE
page 15
1 Seattle, Washington
2 *Answers will vary.*
3 *Answers will vary.*

WATCH AND LISTEN

Exercise 1 page 16
Answers will vary.

Exercise 2 page 16
1 Charleston, South Carolina
2 *Answers will vary.*
3 *Answers will vary.*

Exercise 3 page 17
1 South
2 San Francisco
3 18
4 surprised
5 horse carriage
6 regulated
7 big
8 billion

Exercise 4 page 17
1 b
2 e
3 d
4 f
5 c
6 a

Exercise 5 page 17
1 *Possible answers:* roof, tower
2 *Possible answers:* a long time, many hundreds
3 *Possible answers:* salesperson, seller
4 *Possible answers:* wagon, cart

Exercise 6 page 17
1 *Possible answers:* the length of the tours, how tourists see the sites and what tourists will see
2 *Possible answers:* the length of the tour, where it starts, when it happens and the times the tours start
3 *Answers will vary.*

READING 1

Exercise 1 page 18
a traffic
b countryside
c modern
d population
e pollution
f capital
g expert
h opportunity

Exercises 2–3 page 18
c

Exercise 4 page 20
1 T
2 T
3 T
4 F; More than 35 cities in the world are megacities.
5 F; Most megacities are in Asia, South America, and Africa.
6 F; Finding a house or an apartment to live in is difficult in megacities.

Exercise 5 page 20
Tokyo – lots of jobs, traffic jams, busy trains, good place to study
Delhi – interesting places to visit, mix of different people, housing problem
Cairo – important industries, good place to study

Exercise 7 page 21
1 2
2 40
3 12
4 8
5 8.7
6 20
7 25
8 4
9 1,200

Exercise 8 page 21
a

Exercise 9 page 21
Answers will vary.

READING 2

Exercise 1 page 22
1 quiet
2 area
3 local
4 cheap
5 downtown
6 expensive
7 noisy

Exercises 2–3 page 22
b

Exercise 4 page 22
Answers will vary.

Exercise 5 page 24
a A Mountain Village
b A House Near the Forest
c A Big City

Exercise 6 page 24
Answers will vary. Suggested answers:
1 The Atal family lives in a ~~city~~ **village**. It is a ~~busy~~ **friendly** place. The mountains are very ~~cold~~ **beautiful**.
2 Kate and Julian Foxton live in the ~~Northeast~~ **Pacific Northwest** of the United States. The area is great for ~~theaters~~ **sports like hiking, kayaking, and mountain biking**. The houses are really ~~cheap~~ **expensive**.
3 Chafic and Aline Halwany live in a ~~small~~ **large** city. People learn ~~English~~ **Arabic** and French in the downtown area. There is a lot of traffic ~~at night~~ **during the day**.

Exercise 7 page 24
Answers will vary.

Exercise 8 page 24
Answers will vary.

LANGUAGE DEVELOPMENT

Exercise 1 page 25
noun – 1, verb – 2, adjective – 3

Exercise 2 page 25
noun – town, café, building
verb – live, drive, have
adjective – excellent, exciting, different

Exercise 3 page 26
1 b
2 a
3 c
4 e
5 d

Exercise 4 page 26
1 polluted
2 expensive
3 quiet
4 interesting
5 ugly

CRITICAL THINKING

Exercise 1 page 27
Reading 1 is about megacities. Reading 2 is about smaller parts of cities, towns, and villages.

Exercise 2 page 27
1 +
2 +
3 –
4 +
5 –
6 +

Exercise 3 page 27
Sort answers in T-chart as identified in Exercise 2.

Exercise 4 page 28
Answers will vary. Possible answers:
Positive – Some cities have great public transportation.
Negative – Some big cities are very expensive.

Exercise 5 page 28
Answers will vary.

Exercise 6 page 28
Answers will vary.

GRAMMAR FOR WRITING

Exercise 1 page 29
1 S – Paris, V – is
2 S – The town, V – does not have
3 S – I, V – live
4 S – Istanbul, V – has
5 S – (Many) students, V – live
6 S – The village, V – is not
7 S – The stores, V – are
8 S – The houses (in the town), V – are not

Exercise 2 page 29
  S V
1 I am Mexican.
  S   V
2 He is / was an engineer.
        S   V
3 The people are / were nice.
    S   V
4 We are / were happy.
      S   V
5 Seattle is / was beautiful.
  S V
6 It is / was a small town.

Exercise 3 page 30

1 aren't
2 is
3 aren't
4 are
5 is
6 aren't

Exercise 4 page 30

2 There is a famous museum in my city.
3 There is not / isn't a lake in my town.
4 There are a lot of cars in my city.
5 There are many expensive stores in my city.
6 There is a quiet park in my town.
7 There are not / aren't many people in my town.

Exercise 5 pages 30–31

2 There are lots of museums.
3 There are twelve universities.
4 There is a port.
5 There is one airport.
6 There are many five-star hotels.
7 There is a castle.
8 There isn't a subway system.

ACADEMIC WRITING SKILLS

Exercise 1 page 31

I live in **Montreal. It** is a city in **Canada. It** is a beautiful city. **There** are many stores and restaurants. **The** people are friendly. **There** is an art festival in **June. People** in **Montreal** speak both **French** and **English. It** is very crowded with tourists in the summer. **In** the winter, people like to ice skate and cross-country ski.

ON CAMPUS

Exercise 2 page 34

shared house	dorm	apartment	homestay
share a bathroom free parking	share a room on campus includes activities	pay a deposit live alone unfurnished pay for parking near campus	take a bus includes meals

UNIT 2
ACTIVATE YOUR KNOWLEDGE

page 37

1 Sydney, Australia; fireworks
2 (left to right) a wedding, a religious celebration, a birthday party
3 South Korea, Saudi Arabia, the United States

WATCH AND LISTEN

Exercise 1 page 38
Answers will vary.

Exercise 2 page 38
Answers will vary.

Exercise 3 page 38
The following appear in the video:
a flag, a costume, a drum, children, a parade, old glasses

Exercise 4 page 39

1 b
2 a
3 b
4 a
5 a

Exercise 5 page 39

1 d
2 e
3 a
4 c
5 b

Exercise 6 page 39
a

Exercise 7 page 39
Answers will vary.

READING 1

Exercise 1 page 40

1 celebrate
2 culture
3 gift
4 traditional
5 lucky
6 the ground

Exercises 2–3 page 40
a

Exercise 4 page 42

1 Mexico
2 China
3 Greece
4 Japan
5 the U.S.

Exercise 5 page 42
1 F; Piñatas have candy inside them.
2 F; Long noodles are lucky in Chinese Culture.
3 F; Mother's Day in the U.S. is the second week in May.
4 T
5 T

Exercise 6 page 42
a

Exercise 7 page 42
photos, length of paragraphs, title, design of the article

Exercise 8 page 42
Answers will vary.

READING 2

Exercise 1 page 43
1 a
2 b
3 a
4 b
5 a
6 b

Exercise 2 page 43
Oman, Muscat Festival, February

Exercise 3 page 44
a 5
b 1
c 4
d 2
e 3

Exercise 4 page 45
1 February
2 visit / attend / enjoy
3 Green Mountain
4 Muscat Art Festival
5 popular
6 *Possible answers:* food; music; the mix of different cultures

Exercise 5 page 45
a

Exercise 6 page 45
Answers will vary. Possible answers:
language, family, religion, art, literature, film, dance, sports, TV

Exercise 7 page 45
Answers will vary.

LANGUAGE DEVELOPMENT

Exercise 1 page 46

	on	in	at
places		a town Istanbul my country Brazil	school home work
times	January 1 Sunday Tuesday	June the evening the morning	night eight o'clock

Exercise 2 page 46
1 at
2 on
3 in
4 on
5 at
6 in
7 at
8 at
9 on

Exercise 3 page 47
Answers will vary.

Exercise 4 page 47
Answers will vary.

Exercise 5 page 47
1 The music usually starts at eight o'clock in the evening.
2 I always eat cake on my birthday.
3 She never forgets to call her family.
4 The children sometimes get money instead of toys.
5 In New York, it often snows in February.

CRITICAL THINKING

Exercise 1 page 48
Suggested answers:
Name: Muscat Festival
When: February, every year
Where: Oman
Food & drinks: different types of food
Activities: look at new products, watch the cycling race, go to the Muscat Art Festival
Clothes: traditional clothes (inferred from photos; no information in text)

Exercises 2–4 page 49
Answers will vary.

GRAMMAR FOR WRITING

Exercise 1 page 50

1 subject: The children; verb: wear
2 subject: My family and I; verb: watch
3 subject: I; verb: visit
4 subject: People in the U.S.; verb: celebrate
5 subject: My parents and I; verb: go

Exercise 2 page 50

1 at home; P
2 beautiful; A
3 presents; N
4 in the evening; P
5 traditional A

Exercise 3 page 51

1 People in Canada celebrate Thanksgiving.
2 My parents and I cook on Sunday.
3 Everyone in my town is excited about the party.
4 My family eats in the morning.
5 We do not visit my grandparents.

Exercise 4 page 51

1 PP: at night, O: concerts
2 PP: In India, O: the Magh Bihu festival
3 PP: in the morning, O: their homes
4 PP: at school, O: parties
5 PP: On Saturday, O: the parades

ACADEMIC WRITING SKILLS

Exercise 1 page 52

c 1
d 1
e 2
f 1
g 1
h 2
i 1

Exercise 2 page 52

T: When I was a child, my favorite day of the year was my birthday.
S: I always went to the park with my family. My sister and brother gave me presents, and we usually played games. We ate lunch, and then for dessert, we ate the chocolate cake my mother made.
C: In sum, I have very special memories of my birthday.

Exercise 3 page 53

a S
b S
c T
d C
e S

Exercise 4 page 53

Students should circle the following:

a lasts two days; people laugh, have fun, forget their troubles.
b ancient; celebrates the beginning of spring
e friends and family get together and throw colored water and powder at each other; celebrates the beautiful colors that come with spring

WRITING TASK

Exercise 1 page 53

1 March
2 17th
3 parade
4 beach
5 paella
6 rice
7 red
8 dress

ON CAMPUS

Exercise 3 page 57

Interculture Club Meet and Greet	Language Exchange	CultureFest	Mount Rainier Field Trip
meets every week free event must be a student includes lunch	meets every week free event students teach something students must sign up	free event students teach something students must sign up	students travel by van includes lunch students must sign up students must pay a fee

UNIT 3
ACTIVATE YOUR KNOWLEDGE

page 59
Answers will vary.

WATCH AND LISTEN

Exercise 1 page 60
Answers will vary.

Exercise 2 page 60
Answers will vary.

Exercise 3 page 61

1 texting
2 talking
3 walking, looking
4 taking
5 showing

Exercise 4 page 61

1 billion
2 money
3 advertising
4 buy
5 quickly
6 customers

Exercise 5 page 61

1 c
2 b
3 a
4 e
5 d

Exercise 6 page 61

Answers will vary.

Exercise 4 page 61

Answers will vary.

READING 1

Exercise 1 page 62

a benefit
b interest
c collect
d free
e security
f record
g software
h secret

Exercise 2 page 62

Title: Tech Expert Today; Subtitle: Someone's Always Watching You Online ...

Exercises 3–4 page 62

b

Exercise 5 page 64

1 take information without asking you
2 different advertisements to different people

Exercise 6 page 64

A your address, your online habits, the websites you visit
B your interests, your gender (male/female), your age
C other websites you might like
D your social media page, a data broker

Exercise 7 page 65

Answers will vary.

Exercise 8 page 65

b, d, e

Exercises 9–11 page 65

Answers will vary.

READING 2

Exercise 1 page 66

1 download
2 educational
3 improve
4 imagination
5 creative
6 affect

Exercise 2 page 66

+: advantage, benefit, positive
–: disadvantage, negative

Exercise 3 page 66

Answers will vary.

Exercise 4 page 68

1 3; However, a recent study suggests that video games can also be bad for children.
2 2; For many people, video games are fun and educational.

Exercise 5 page 68

(+) cross outs: 3 teach children about money; 5 can help children exercise.
(–) cross outs: 7 are boring; 10 can cause problems between parents and children.

Exercise 6 page 68

1 a
2 c

Exercise 7 page 68

Answers will vary.

LANGUAGE DEVELOPMENT

Exercise 1 page 69

1 d
2 e
3 b
4 f
5 a
6 c

Exercise 2 page 69

1 keyboard
2 smartphone
3 email address
4 Web page
5 video game
6 computer program

Exercise 3 page 70

d

Exercises 4–5 page 70

Answers will vary.

CRITICAL THINKING

Exercise 1 page 71

1 b

2 a

Exercise 2 page 71

Computers help us do work:

You can get help from different websites.

You can read newspapers from around the world.

People can work at home sometimes.

You can read your email.

You can watch educational videos.

You can learn new words in a different language.

Computers waste our time:

You could lose valuable information if your computer breaks.

You can visit social networking sites.

You can play video games.

You could get addicted to technology.

Exercises 3–4 page 72

Answers will vary.

GRAMMAR FOR WRITING

Exercise 1 page 73

2 You can share photos and talk to your friends.

3 I use online banking and check my email.

4 She does homework and watches movies on her computer.

5 I often shop for clothes on the Internet and pay with my credit card.

Exercise 2 page 73

Second sentences:

1 They also download videos.

2 I read a lot of travel blogs, too.

3 I also check social media.

4 I also look at photos on my smartphone.

Exercise 3 page 74

2 I sent an email to Alan, but he did not write me back.

3 I like to shop online, but my father thinks it's not safe.

4 I call my mother every Saturday, and I visit her every Sunday.

5 I bought a new phone, but it doesn't work.

6 You can check the weather, and you can find a good restaurant.

7 Some games are educational, but other games are just for fun.

Exercise 4 page 74

2 a Many apps help people with their work, but some apps are a waste of time.

b Many apps help people with their work. However, some apps are a waste of time.

3 a I use online banking, but I sometimes forget my password.

b I use online banking. However, I sometimes forget my password.

4 a I use the Internet on my smartphone, but sometimes it is very slow.

b I use the Internet on my smartphone. However, sometimes it is very slow.

ACADEMIC WRITING SKILLS

Exercise 1 page 75

Paragraph 2: For many people, video games are fun and educational.

Paragraph 3: However, a recent study suggests that video games can also be bad for children.

Exercise 2 page 75

1 topic: social networking sites; controlling idea: make it easy to keep in touch with your friends

2 topic: smartphones; controlling idea: can be expensive

3 topic: information on the Internet; controlling idea: is not reliable

4 topic: information online; controlling idea: You can access [it] from all over the world.

Exercise 3 page 75

a Smartphones can be expensive.

b You can access information online from all over the world.

c Social media sites make it easy to keep in touch with your friends.

d Information on the Internet is not reliable.

ON CAMPUS

Exercise 3 page 79

1 T

2 F

3 F

4 F

5 T

Exercise 4 page 79

Response 1: a

Response 2: c

Response 3: d

Response 4: b

UNIT 4
ACTIVATE YOUR KNOWLEDGE
page 81
1 a sun
  b wind
  c rain
  d snow
2–3 *Answers will vary.*
4 fog

WATCH AND LISTEN

Exercises 1–2 page 82
Answers will vary.

Exercise 3 page 82
1 Alley
2 2011
3 160
4 cannot
5 weather
6 twenty-five
7 difficult

Exercise 4 page 83
1 b
2 c
3 a
4 e
5 d

Exercise 5 page 83
b

Exercise 6 page 83
Yes, they enjoy their work. They sound very excited when they find the right tornado. They risk their lives to do their jobs.

Exercises 7–8 page 83
Answers will vary.

READING 1

Exercise 1 page 84
1 cover
2 lightning
3 Almost
4 last
5 thunder
6 huge
7 dangerous

Exercise 2 page 84
1 *Answers will vary.*
2 *Extreme* means the most unusual or the most serious possible.
3 *Possible answers:* tornadoes, hurricanes, droughts, sandstorms, etc.

Exercise 3 page 86
1 a
2 b
3 a
4 b
5 a

Exercise 4 page 86
1 b
2 a
3 a
4 b

Exercise 5 page 86
1 b
2 c
3 a

Exercise 6 page 87
Answers will vary.

READING 2

Exercise 1 page 87
1 b
2 a

Exercise 2 page 87
a careful
b drop
c decide
d shock
e rise
f precipitation

Exercise 3 page 88
Answers will vary.

Exercise 4 page 88
a 8
b 6
c 4
d 7
e 5

Exercise 5 page 88
1 d
2 c
3 a
4 b

Exercise 6 page 88
b

Exercises 7–9 page 88
Answers will vary.

LANGUAGE DEVELOPMENT

Exercise 1 page 90
1 high
2 low
3 maximum
4 minimum

Exercise 2 page 90
1 A
2 B
3 A
4 B
5 B
6 A

Exercise 3 page 91
1 rise(s), reach(es)
2 fall(s), drop(s)

Exercise 4 page 91
1 **a** an increase
  b reaches
2 **a** a decrease
  b drops
3 **a** a decrease
  b falls to
4 **a** an increase
  b rises

CRITICAL THINKING

Exercise 1 page 92
1 temperatures
2 times
3 maximum temperature in the day
4 minimum temperature in the day

Exercise 2 page 92
Answers will vary. Possible answers:
The graphs show information on temperature and precipitation in Anchorage and Amman throughout the year.

Exercise 3 page 93
1 precipitation in inches and millimeters
2 temperature in Fahrenheit and Celsius
3 Amman
4 average temperatures
5 bar graphs
6 line graphs

Exercise 4 page 93
Anchorage, Alaska

	Jan	Feb	Mar	Apr	May	Jun
precipitation	.75 in (19 mm)	.71 in (18 mm)	.59 in (15 mm)	.47 in (12 mm)	.71 in (18 mm)	.98 in (25 mm)
avg high temp	23°F (-5°C)	27°F (-3°C)	34°F (1°C)	44°F (7°C)	56°F (13°C)	63°F (17°C)
avg low temp	11°F (12°C)	14°F (-10°C)	19°F (-7°C)	29°F (-2°C)	40°F (4°C)	48°F (9°C)

	Jul	Aug	Sept	Oct	Nov	Dec
precipitation	1.81 in (46 mm)	3.27 in (83 mm)	2.99 in (76 mm)	2.05 in (52 mm)	1.14 in (29 mm)	1.1 in (28 mm)
avg high temp	65°F (18°C)	64°F (17°C)	55°F (18°C)	40°F (4°C)	28°F (-2°C)	25°F (-4°C)
avg low temp	52°F (11°C)	50°F (10°C)	42°F (6°C)	29°F (-2°C)	17°F (-8°C)	13°F (-11°C)

Amman, Jordan

	Jan	Feb	Mar	Apr	May	Jun
precipitation	2.3 in (58 mm)	1.5 in (37 mm)	1.9 in (49 mm)	0.6 in (16 mm)	0.6 in (16 mm)	0 in (0 mm)
avg high temp	54°F (12°C)	55°F (13°C)	63°F (17°C)	73°F (23°C)	82°F (28°C)	88°F (31°C)
avg low temp	39°F (4°C)	39°F (4°C)	45°F (7°C)	52°F (11°C)	59°F (15°C)	64°F (18°C)

	Jul	Aug	Sept	Oct	Nov	Dec
precipitation	0.07 in (2 mm)	0.7 in (18 mm)	0.3 in (7 mm)	0.7 in (18 mm)	1.5 in (38 mm)	1.4 in (35 mm)
avg high temp	90°F (32°C)	91°F (33°C)	88°F (31°C)	81°F (27°C)	68°F (20°C)	59°F (15°C)
avg low temp	68°F (20°C)	68°F (20°C)	64°F (18°C)	59°F (15°C)	50°F (10°C)	43°F (6°C)

Exercise 5 page 93
Answers will vary.

Exercise 6 page 93
1 Anchorage: July; Amman: August
2 Anchorage: January; Amman: January and February
3 Anchorage: August; Amman: January
4 Anchorage: April; Amman: June
5 *Answers will vary.*
6 Anchorage: snow; Amman: drought
7 Anchorage: problems with transportation; Amman: limited food

GRAMMAR FOR WRITING

Exercise 1 page 95
colder; coldest
lower; lowest
more extreme; most extreme
drier; driest
bigger; biggest
easier; easiest

Exercise 2 page 96
1 higher
2 colder
3 lowest
4 wetter
5 drier
6 rainiest
7 sunny

ACADEMIC WRITING SKILLS

Exercise 1 page 96
1 Main idea: The hottest time is between 2 p.m. and 4 p.m.
  Data: Temperatures rise to 91°F (33°C).
2 Main idea: The coldest time is at 4 a.m.
  Data: Temperatures fall to 30°F (-1°C).

Exercise 2 page 96
1 a
2 b

Exercise 3 page 97
1 c
2 b
3 a
4 d

Exercise 4 page 97
a, b, d, f

Exercise 5 page 98
Answers will vary. Suggested answers:
2 It is too hot to snow in some U.S. cities, like Las Vegas and Miami.
  It is too hot to snow in some U.S. cities, such as Las Vegas and Miami.
  It is too hot to snow in some U.S. cities, for example, Las Vegas and Miami.
3 There are a lot of tornadoes in certain cities, like Oklahoma and Texas.
  There are a lot of tornadoes in certain cities, such as Oklahoma and Texas.
  There are a lot of tornadoes in certain cities, for example, Oklahoma and Texas.

4 When you go camping, bring important items like water and sunblock.
  When you go camping, bring important items, such as water and sunblock.
  When you go camping, bring important items, for example, water and sunblock.

ON CAMPUS

Exercise 2 page 100
1 emergency room
2 photo ID; insurance card
3 translator
4 Travel Clinic

UNIT 5
ACTIVATE YOUR KNOWLEDGE

page 103
1 a triathlon
2–5 *Answers will vary.*

WATCH AND LISTEN

Exercise 1 page 104
Answers will vary. Possible answers:
1 skiing, mountain climbing, hiking, mountain biking
2 running, swimming, skiing
3 skiing, skating, sledding

Exercise 2 page 104
Answers will vary.

Exercise 3 page 104
1 popular
2 best
3 well-known
4 rich
5 blue

Exercise 4 page 105
1 swimmer: skier
2 two: four
3 is: isn't
4 up: down
5 minute: second
6 slow: fast

Exercise 5 page 105
a 3
b 2
c 4
d 1

Exercise 6 page 105
Answers will vary.

Exercise 7 page 105
Answers will vary.

Exercise 8 page 105
Answers will vary. Possible answers:
baseball: bat, ball, helmet, glove, field
ice hockey: skates, hockey stick, puck, helmet, ice
cycling: bike, helmet
soccer: soccer shoes, soccer ball, net, field
fishing: fishing pole, tackle box, worms
swimming: swim suit, water/pool, goggles
golf: clubs, golfing shoes, balls, golf course
tennis: racket, tennis balls, net, tennis court

READING 1

Exercise 1 page 106
1 take place
2 race
3 ancient
4 strange
5 throw
6 competition
7 swimming

Exercises 2–3 page 107
1 b
2 b
3 a, b, and d

Exercise 4 page 109
a Paragraph 5
b Paragraph 3
c Paragraph 6
d Paragraph 4
e Paragraph 2

Exercise 5 page 109
1 Indonesia
2 Singapore, China, Malaysia, Indonesia
3 Turkey
4 Scotland
5 the U.S.

Exercise 6 page 109
1 The Coney Island Polar Bear Plunge takes place every Sunday from October to April and on New Year's Day.
2 The Coney Island Polar Bear Plunge began in 1903.
3 A dragon boat has a dragon's head painted on it.
4 There are 22 people in each dragon boat team.
5 A caber is a large piece of wood.
6 A caber is usually the size of a small tree.
7 In fireball soccer, the ball is made from coconut shells.

8 The ball is on fire throughout a game of fireball soccer.
9 The Ephesus camel wrestling competition happens once a year.
10 In camel wrestling, two male camels fight each other.

Exercise 7 page 110
1 a
2 b
3 b

Exercise 8 page 110
Answers will vary.

READING 2

Exercise 1 page 110
1 a
2 a
3 b
4 a
5 b
6 b

Exercise 2 page 111
a newspaper article

Exercise 3 page 111
Answers will vary. Possible answers:
a competition, a difficult race

Exercise 5 page 111
1 difficult
2 cold
3 countries
4 get hurt
5 strong
6 different

Exercise 6 page 111
1 d
2 f
3 e
4 b
5 a
6 c

Exercise 7 page 113
1 the U.K.
2 January
3 9 miles (15 kilometers)
4 all year
5 because it is exciting and challenging

Exercise 8 page 113
1 c, e
2 b, d
3 a, f

Exercise 9 page 113
1 a
2 a

Exercise 10 page 113
Answers will vary.

Exercise 11 page 113
Answers will vary.

LANGUAGE DEVELOPMENT

Exercise 1 page 114
1 f
2 g
3 c
4 b
5 e
6 d
7 a

Exercise 2 page 114
1 along
2 past
3 over/across
4 across/through
5 under
6 through
7 across
8 around/along

CRITICAL THINKING

Exercise 1 page 115
1 bridge
2 swim route
3 tunnel
4 bike route
5 central library
6 running route

Exercise 2 page 116
1 6.2 miles (10 kilometers)
2 1 mile (1,500 meters)
3 25 miles (40 kilometers)

Exercise 3 page 116
a over/across
b through
c along
d across
e past

Exercise 4 page 116
a 4
b 3
c 5
d 1
e 2

GRAMMAR FOR WRITING

Exercise 1 page 116
1 subject: The boys and girls, verb: play
2 subject: The whole family, verb: watches
3 subject: Aisha, verb: runs
4 subject: Soccer, verb: is
5 subject: The racers, verb: run
6 subject: Hanh and I, verb: love

Exercise 2 page 117
1 is
2 swims
3 rides
4 wins
5 practice
6 is

Exercise 3 page 117
1 try
2 carries
3 is
4 watch
5 miss
6 wants
7 run
8 are
9 catch

ACADEMIC WRITING SKILLS

Exercise 1 page 118
1 b
2 d
3 c
4 a

Exercise 2 page 118
1 First, the weightlifter lifts the weight onto his shoulders.
2 Second, the weightlifter lifts the weight above his head.
3 Third, the weightlifter holds the weight above his head for as long as he can.
4 Finally, the weightlifter drops the weight to the ground.

Exercise 3 page 118
Answers will vary. Sample answer:
The tennis players walk onto the court. Next, they pick up their racquets. Then, one player hits the ball over the net. After that, the other player hits the ball back.

Exercise 5 page 119

The high jump is an Olympic sport that is practiced in many countries. ~~Athletes competed in over 30 venues during the 2012 London Olympic Games.~~ First, the high jumper runs toward the bar. It is important to run very fast. ~~The high jump is the most popular sport in Russia.~~ Second, the high jumper jumps. ~~I was on the track and field team at school.~~ The high jumper must jump from the right foot and keep their arms close to their sides. Next, the high jumper twists their body so their back is to the bar. They must lift their head and feet and keep them high above the bar. ~~The high jump is a really interesting sport.~~ After that, the high jumper lands. They must be careful to land safely on the mat. ~~Derek Drouin from Canada won the gold medal in the men's high jump at the 2016 Rio Olympic Games, and Ruth Beitia from Spain won the gold for the women's high jump.~~ Finally, the high jumper stands up, takes a bow and leaves the mat.

WRITING TASK

Exercise 1 page 120

A *Answers will vary.*

B 1 swim across the lake
   2 ride a bike past the library
   3 ride a bike through the tunnel
   4 ride a bike over/across the bridge
   5 run along the road

ON CAMPUS

Exercise 3 page 122

1 DNS
2 T
3 DNS
4 T
5 T
6 F

UNIT 6
ACTIVATE YOUR KNOWLEDGE

page 125

1 a top: Bill Gates; bottom: Mark Zuckerberg
  b Microsoft, Facebook
  c *Answers will vary.*

2–3 *Answers will vary.*

WATCH AND LISTEN

Exercise 1 page 126
Answers will vary.

Exercises 2–3 page 126
Statement 1 is true.

Exercise 4 page 126
1, 2, 3, 4, 5, 6, 7, 8, 9, 10

Exercise 5 page 127
1 Seattle
2 100
3 website
4 large
5 fulfillment

Exercise 6 page 127
1 T
2 F
3 F
4 T
5 T

Exercise 7 page 127
a 5
b 3
c 2
d 1
e 4

Exercise 8 page 127
b

Exercise 9 page 127
Answers will vary.

READING 1

Exercise 1 page 128
1 a
2 b
3 a
4 b
5 b
6 a

Exercises 2–3 page 128
1 b
2 a

Exercise 4 page 130
There are ~~three~~ *four* main kinds of work – work with ~~animals~~ *people*, work with information, work with ~~machines~~ *things*, and work with ideas. The quiz helps you to find out about the kind of ~~people~~ *jobs* you might like. After the quiz, you read the advice to find ~~universities~~ *jobs* you may like.

Exercise 5–6 page 130
Answers will vary.

Exercise 8 page 130
1 a
2 a
3 b
4 a

Exercise 9 page 131

b, c

Exercise 10 page 131

Answers will vary.

READING 2

Exercise 1 page 131

a introduce
b office
c run
d partner
e goal
f employ
g set up
h advertise

Exercise 2 page 132

Google, business, entrepreneurs

Exercise 4 page 132

a 3
b 1
c 2

Exercise 5 page 132

1 b
2 a
3 a
4 a

Exercise 6 page 134

1 F; Google has three man focuses: to make their search
 engine fast and smart, to develop products that can
 work on different devices and in different places,
 and to help new businesses advertise and find new
 customers.
2 T
3 T
4 F; Google released a program that allows people to see
 famous works of art.

Exercise 7 page 134

a A: 2000; B: 2
b A: 2008; B: 4
c A: 1997; B: 1
d A: 2005; B: 3

Exercise 8 page 134

a

Exercise 9 page 134

3

Exercise 10 page 134

Answers will vary.

Exercise 11 page 135

1 creative
2 *Answers will vary.*

LANGUAGE DEVELOPMENT

Exercise 1 page 135

a N
b N
c V
d N
e V
f V

Exercise 2 page 135

1 plan
2 Expand
3 partner
4 Run
5 Set up
6 contact

Exercise 3 page 135

1 before
2 after

Exercise 4 page 136

1 b
2 e
3 c
4 a
5 d

Exercise 5 page 136

1 employees
2 office
3 software
4 employ
5 products

CRITICAL THINKING

Exercise 1 page 137

Answers will vary.

Exercise 3 page 137

a 2005
b 1998
c 1997
d 1995
e 2008
f 2006
g 2000
h 2011

Exercises 4–5 page 138

Answers will vary.

GRAMMAR FOR WRITING

Exercise 3 page 139

1 is; present
2 joined; past
3 is; present
4 became; past
5 bought; past
6 celebrated; past

Exercise 2 page 139

1 sells
2 set up
3 did
4 employed
5 expanded
6 opened
7 is

Exercise 3 page 140

1 is
2 opened
3 sells
4 is
5 started
6 sold
7 makes
8 designed

Exercise 4 page 140

1 She became the CEO when she was 30. / When she was 30, she became the CEO.
2 They employed six new workers when the business expanded. / When the business expanded, they employed six new workers.
3 He left his job when he was 65. / When he was 65, he left his job.
4 The store closed when the economy crashed. / When the economy crashed, the store closed.
5 They expanded the company when it was still successful. / When it was still successful, they expanded the company.

ACADEMIC WRITING SKILLS

Exercise 1 page 141

1 a
2 d
3 b
4 c

Exercise 2 page 142

1 a
2 d
3 b
4 e
5 c
6 g
7 h
8 f

ON CAMPUS

Exercise 3 page 145

1 Hiroo
2 Anya
3 Karl
4 Anya
5 Hiroo

Exercise 4 page 145

American Literature 112
2 write summary of short story
3 library: get information about author
4 choose novel for final paper
Math 114
3 do Problem Set 4
4 review algebra formulas for midterm
To-do
2 buy airline ticket for spring break
3 make dentist appointment
4 get haircut

UNIT 7

ACTIVATE YOUR KNOWLEDGE

page 147

1 Mahatma Gandhi, Barack Obama, and Diana, Princess of Wales
2 Mahatma Gandhi (1869–1948) was a leader of the Indian independence movement. He led protests against British rule, using non-violent methods of civil disobedience (i.e., breaking rules without hurting people). He is known in India as the Father of the Nation. He was assassinated in 1948, shortly after India declared independence.
Barack Obama (1961–) is the first African American president of the U.S. He was the president from January 2009 through January 2017. He attended Harvard Law School, and he won the Nobel Peace Prize in 2009.
Diana, Princess of Wales (1961–1997) was married to Prince Charles, the heir to the British throne. She was known for her work for various charities. She divorced Prince Charles in 1996 and died in a car crash in Paris the following year.

WATCH AND LISTEN

Exercise 1 page 148
Answers will vary.

Exercise 2 page 148
Answers will vary.

Exercise 3 page 149
1 F; 8,500 volunteers record the weather in the U.S. every day.
2 T
3 F; He monitors the temperature from his backyard.
4 F; This job is easy for him.
5 F; Richard also checks the rainfall daily.
6 T
7 T

Exercise 4 page 149
1 c
2 a
3 b
4 b

Exercise 5 page 149
Answers will vary.

Exercise 6 page 149
Answers will vary.

READING 1

Exercise 1 page 150
1 operation
2 incredible
3 blind
4 talent
5 respect
6 inspire

Exercise 2 page 150
c

Exercise 4 page 152
a 3
b 1
c 4
d 2

Exercise 5 page 152
1 T
2 F; He was different to most other teenagers.
3 F; He learned to "see" with his ears.
4 F; Ben loved riding his bicycle.
5 T
6 T

Exercise 6 page 152
1 b
2 e
3 a
4 c
5 g
6 d
7 f

Exercise 7 page 153
b

Exercise 8 page 153
1 b
2 b

Exercise 9 page 153
Answers will vary.

READING 2

Exercise 1 page 154
a dream
b take care of
c brave
d former
e intelligent
f train
g honest
h achieve

Exercise 2 page 156
1 c
2 a
3 d
4 b

Exercise 3 page 156
1 In 2009, the Singapore Women's Everest team climbed Everest after ~~five~~ *seven* years of training.
2 Malala Yousafzai donated $1.1 million to build a ~~library~~ *school* in Pakistan.
3 Steve Jobs died in ~~June~~ *October* 2011.
4 Mark's mother takes care of his ~~grandmother~~ *nephew* in the hospital.

Exercise 4 page 156
a 3
b 2
c 1
d 4

Exercise 5 page 156
Answers will vary.

Exercise 6 page 157
Answers will vary.

LANGUAGE DEVELOPMENT

Exercise 1 page 157
1 c
2 d
3 g
4 e
5 f
6 a
7 b

Exercise 2 page 157
1 She is the new leader of the country.
2 I met a friend of my brother's.
3 My mother gave me a piece of cake.
4 A dentist is a kind of doctor.
5 He is the former director of technology.

Exercise 3 page 158
positive: reliable, confident, honest, calm, talented, kind, shy, intelligent, patient, clever, sensible, friendly
negative: lazy, shy, stupid, difficult, selfish
Note: *Shy* can be seen as both positive and negative, according to the effect that shyness has on a particular person and in a particular situation.

Exercise 4 page 158
1 honest
2 calm
3 friendly
4 shy
5 lazy
6 reliable
7 sensible
8 talented

CRITICAL THINKING

Exercise 1 page 159
Answers will vary.

Exercise 2 page 160
a Singapore Women's Everest Team
b Mary Evans, Malala Yousafzai
c Steve Jobs, Malala Yousafzai
d Steve Jobs

Exercises 3–7 page 160–161
Answers will vary.

GRAMMAR FOR WRITING

Exercise 1 page 161
1 Good role models should / must / have to work hard.
2 Good role models should not / must not / do not have to be selfish.
3 Good role models should / must / have to ask others what they need.
4 Good role models should / must / have to be patient.
5 Good role models should not / must not / do not have to be mean to others.

Exercise 2 page 162
1 It is important to be patient.
2 It is important to spend time with your family.
3 It is important to learn about other people.
4 It is important to get a good education.
5 It is important to be reliable.

Exercise 3 page 162
Answers will vary.

ACADEMIC WRITING SKILLS

Exercise 1 page 162
a

Exercise 2 page 162
In summary

Exercise 3 page 162
b

Exercise 4 page 163
1 d
2 c
3 b
4 a

Exercise 5 page 163
b

ON CAMPUS

Exercise 2 page 166
1 a
2 c
3 b

Exercise 3 page 166
1 should not
2 doesn't agree
3 thinks
4 writes
5 understands

Exercise 4 page 167

Erica: <u>In my opinion</u>, uniforms are not good for high school students. They should be able to choose their own clothes. Clothes are important for teenagers because they want to have their own style.

Renee: That's a good point Erica. However, <u>I feel</u> uniforms are better for everyone. Some students can afford nice clothes, but some students can't buy those clothes. <u>I believe</u> uniforms make everyone the same at school.

David: I agree, Renee. <u>I think</u> school should be for studying, not for fashion. Erica, I see your point but I don't really agree. Can't students wear their own clothes after school?

Exercise 5 page 167

1 think
2 opinion
3 agree
4 see
5 but

UNIT 8
ACTIVATE YOUR KNOWLEDGE

page 169
1 The person is fixing equipment on a spacecraft.
2–3 *Answers will vary.*

WATCH AND LISTEN

Exercise 1 page 170
Answers will vary.

Exercise 2 page 170
Answers will vary.

Exercise 3 page 171
1 She is an astronaut.
2 The International Space Station
3 She gets there in a rocket.
4 traffic
5 Her drive to work.

Exercise 4 page 171
1 15–20
2 two
3 four
4 250
5 nine

Exercise 5 page 171
1 This rocket is ~~American~~ Russian.
2 The trip took ~~double~~ half the time it takes her to drive to work.
3 She traveled in a ~~big~~ tiny capsule.
4 She went with a Russian cosmonaut and a ~~Korean~~ Japanese astronaut.
5 They rode the elevator to the ~~bottom~~ top.

Exercise 6 page 171
Answers will vary.

READING 1

Exercise 1 page 172
a entrepreneur
b advances
c private
d explore
e beyond
f crash
g public

Exercise 2 page 172
Answers will vary.

Exercise 3 page 174
1 the era when governments began sending spacecraft into space
2 to make new discoveries in space, especially on Mars
3 take people to the moon and back, take people to mars
4 Private companies don't rely on money from the government.

Exercise 4 page 174
1 F; The Soviet Union sent Sputnik I into space, and it was the first successful spacecraft to orbit the Earth.
2 F; Entrepreneurs like Elon Musk and Richard Branson don't have to wait for government money in order to construct new spacecraft.
3 F; In 2016, a SpaceX spacecraft crashed in the Mojave Desert and killed it pilot.
4 T
5 DNS

Exercise 5 page 174
1 b
2 a
3 b

Exercise 6 page 175
Answers will vary.

READING 2

Exercise 1 page 175
1 a
2 b
3 b
4 a
5 a
6 b
7 b
8 a

Exercise 2 page 176
b

Exercise 3 page 176
a 2
b 4
c 1
d 3

Exercise 4 page 176
1 thousands
2 the Kepler telescope
3 a planet (that is similar to Earth)
4 Princeton University
5 scientific evidence

Exercise 5 page 178
Answers will vary. Possible answers:
because the telescope that discovered it is called Kepler
because it is the 22nd system that was discovered
because it orbits a star that is called 22a

Exercise 6 page 178
1 O
2 F
3 O
4 F

Exercise 7 page 178
1 b
2 b
3 a

Exercise 8 page 178
Answers will vary.

Exercise 9 page 178
Answers will vary.

LANGUAGE DEVELOPMENT

Exercise 1 page 179
1 expert
2 report, study
3 research

Exercise 2 page 179
1 think/believe
2 show/suggest
3 think/believe
4 show/suggest
5 shows/suggests

CRITICAL THINKING

Exercise 1 page 180
the author does not believe that there is life on other planets.

Exercise 2 page 180
paragraph 2: Experts with the best technology can see no signs of life there. Until there is hard evidence, we cannot use Kepler 22b to support the idea of life on other planets.
paragraph 3: Earth has the perfect conditions for life, and it is very unlikely that another planet has exactly the same environment as Earth. ... In addition, although scientists believe that life might exist on other planets, they have never found evidence to prove it.

Exercise 3 page 180
A Governments around the world should spend more money on space programs.
B There are better ways money can be spent, so governments shouldn't spend more money on space exploration.
C Uncovering the mysteries of space is a huge task that should continue to be funded. / Therefore, the government should spend more money on space programs.

Exercise 4 page 182
for: brings countries together (A), astronauts take part in important experiments (A), is necessary for long-term space journeys (to Mars) (A), proves countries can work together (A), make technological advances (C), encourages young people to study science and engineering (C), results in medical advances (C), improves life on Earth by doing research in space (C)
against: expensive (B), dangerous (B), wastes natural resources (B), spends money that should be used on other things that people need (clean water and food, access to education, medical research) (B)

Exercises 5–7 page 182
Answers will vary.

GRAMMAR FOR WRITING

Exercise 1 page 184

1 Scientists believe that we could be living on the moon by 2050.
2 Reports show that Pluto is not a planet.
3 Some people think that TV shows are a good way to learn about science.
4 Studies suggest that life could exist on other planets.

Exercise 2 page 184

Answers will vary. Possible answers:

2 Sir Richard Branson thinks that regular people should have the opportunity to travel in space.
3 The researchers at Princeton University doubt that alien life exists.
4 NASA stated that the Kepler telescope looks for livable planets beyond Earth.

Exercise 3 page 184

1 b
2 c
3 a

Exercise 4 page 184

Answers will vary.

ACADEMIC WRITING SKILLS

Exercise 1 page 185

1 first
2 middle
3 one
4 last

Exercise 2 page 185

1 **background information:** For many years, people have wondered whether we are the only living things in the universe. Some scientists believe that there must be life on other planets because the universe is so big. However, it is unlikely that there is life on other planets because planets need a very specific environment for life to start.
thesis statement: In the end, there are facts no facts that support the idea of life on other planets.

2 **facts, reasons, and examples:** the universe is huge; billions of stars and thousands of solar systems; more than 2,300 planets in orbit around stars; one of these planets, named Kepler 22b has the right conditions – the right atmosphere and temperature – to have life a planet needs very particular conditions to have life; it is very unlikely that another planet has exactly the same environment as Earth; although scientists believe that life might exist on other planets, they have never found evidence to prove it; a recent report from Princeton University suggests that it is very unlikely that there is life on other planets; we don't have enough scientific evidence to decide if there is life on other planets; just because similar conditions to Earth exist on other planets, it doesn't mean that life could exist

3 **phrases that retell the main points in the essay:** Although the universe is very big, a planet with life needs very special conditions; I do not think any other planets could have exactly the same conditions as Earth.
the writer's opinion: In conclusion, I do not believe that there is life on other planets. / Therefore, I do not think that there could be life on other planets.

WRITING TASK

Exercise 1 page 186

a 2 and 3
b 3
c 1 and 3
d *Answers will vary.*

ON CAMPUS

Exercise 2 page 188

1 a
2 a
3 b
4 a

Exercise 3 page 188

1 F
2 F
3 T
4 T
5 F
6 T

STUDENT'S BOOK SCRIPTS

UNIT 1

▶ The Top U.S. City

Reporter: Called the Holy City, for its many church steeples, peaked above the city's low-slung skyline, it beat out San Francisco, which had won the award 18 years in a row.
I think people, at times, are surprised to hear that. Charleston Mayor, Joe Riley.

Joe Riley: Well, you know, when people come to Charleston, whether they're from the U.S. or from another continent, for the first time, they're always surprised. It's like they didn't know this kind of place existed in America.

Reporter: Charleston was a cradle of the Confederacy. It was here the first shots of the Civil War were fired. That history can be felt all around, from streets paved in stones, once used as ballast in sailing ships, to centuries-old houses that line the battery, to the city market, where vendors still sell their handmade crafts. And that doesn't even touch on the great southern cuisine. These are the draws for visitors to Charleston, where the thrill rides don't occur on twisting scream machines, but rather on more sedate vehicles.

Joe Riley: We regulate very carefully the tourism industry. We regulate the number of carriages, where they go. We regulate where buses can go. We regulate the size of walking tours.

Reporter: All that attention to tourism is because it's big business here. 4 million visitors pump more than 3 billion dollars a year into the local economy.

Tom Doyle: Here we go.

Reporter: Tom Doyle has been leading carriage tours in Charleston for more than 30 years.
The attention that Charleston is getting right now, does that surprise you?

Tom Doyle: Uh, no, it doesn't. It surprises me it took as long as it did.
You can go down any street here, look to your left and look to your right and see even more beautiful streets. You can make Charleston your own special place. Isn't this a great city?

Reporter: It's beautiful, I have to say.

UNIT 2

▶ The Meaning of Independence Day

Reporter: To kick off your Fourth of July celebration, how 'bout a little trip to Philadelphia, home of the Second Continental Congress. We found some young Americans in Philly who are learning about the nation's early days from some rather familiar faces.

Men: We hold these truths to be self-evident, that all men are created equal.

Man 1: The Fourth of July is very significant. It is the date upon which we approved the Declaration of Independence.

Woman: I believe that it symbolizes the great unity of our colonies, our collective effort to create our own constellation, our own country.

Young man 1: I think of collaboration, I think of, uh, kind of the best of America, where people—well, the delegates debated together and they really wanted to send a strong message to Britain.
It's really—you know, it's a great day to be American.

Boy 1: Well, I like all the fireworks, and all that's really fun and stuff.

Girl 1: Fireworks.

Girl 2: Our neighbors, like, buy like whole entire box of fireworks, and then they take them and they put them by the sewer and they light them.

Boy 2: Well, the fireworks and it's really fun, but it's like remembering all the people that laid down their lives for us.

Young woman: And I think it's such an important day for us as a nation to celebrate and remember every year. And I think it's so uniting too, to really remember what we were founded on and how blessed we are as a nation.

Young man 2: The sacrifice it took to make this nation and the opportunity we have that many people around the world don't have to life, liberty, and the pursuit of happiness. It's really a neat opportunity to remember how blessed we are to be in this country.

UNIT 3

▶ Predictive Advertising

Narrator: Every time we make a phone call, search online, or buy something, we leave information, or data, about our habits. And the amount of data is getting bigger by 2.5 billion gigabytes every day. All that data is worth a lot of money.

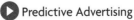

Mike Baker is a "data hunter." He collects data. He thinks this information is changing the way we live and the way we do business.

A few years ago, Mike decided to help advertisers. Why should companies wait for people to find their ads when it was now possible to bring personalized ads to everyone?

Then he had another idea. If companies had enough information about people's past activities, could they use this information to predict their future activities?

Mike felt that they could—that they could predict what people might want to buy. But it was difficult because there was too much data. He needed a program to understand and use the data.

And he wanted to be able to use the data fast—to be able to predict what people wanted to buy, before they even knew it. But he needed help.

So Mike found a partner with a superfast program. Together, they made the program do what Mike wanted it to do. The program looks at data very quickly and finds clues about what people might want to buy.

Then it sends them personalized ads. For example, it might learn that you like Italian food and are interested in cars, so it sends you ads about those things.

We now live in a world of personalized ads. Yes, you can choose not to have personalized ads, but you can't get away from ads completely. So maybe it's better to see ads for things you like than for things you don't care about.

UNIT 4

 Tornadoes

Narrator: In the middle of the United States, spring brings warm, wet air from the south, making things perfect for one of the most extreme weather events on Earth—tornadoes. That's why this part of the country is called Tornado Alley.

Some years are worse than others, and 2011 was one of the worst ever.

Man: Did you see that? The whole house came apart! Oh my God! Oh my God!

Narrator: That year, in the town of Joplin, Missouri, a dangerous tornado killed more than 160 people.

But although we know a lot about the science of tornadoes, we still can't predict exactly when or where they will happen.

Josh Wurman is a weather scientist. He and his team are studying how thunderstorms produce tornadoes.

Seventy-five percent of thunderstorms don't produce tornadoes, but twenty-five percent of them do. But which thunderstorms will do it?

To answer this question, Josh and his team need to get information from as many tornadoes as they can during the spring. To find the storms, Josh uses a Doppler radar scanner. It can show him what's going on inside a thunderstorm, which gives him important information about what starts a tornado.

Josh now knows where to look, but finding the right storm is always difficult. Then, after 1,000 miles of driving, they find the right one. But the team has to move fast because tornadoes come and go very quickly.

And there's the tornado they're looking for.

Woman: There we go. That's what it's about.

Man 1: Yeah.

Man 2: There she is.

Man 1: It's a beauty.

Man 2: It's a beauty.

Man on radio: Be careful. Be careful.

Narrator: This huge tornado is less than a mile away from the team.

Its winds are spinning up to 200 miles per hour.

But less than 30 minutes after the tornado appeared, it dies. It was one of more than 1,200 tornadoes in this part of Tornado Alley since the beginning of spring.

UNIT 5

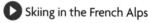 Skiing in the French Alps

Narrator: This is Courchevel, France. It's popular with skiers. There are four villages, and the names tell you the height in meters, like Courchevel 1,300 and Courchevel 1,850, which is the highest most well-known. Rich and famous people, like the American movie star Leonardo DiCaprio, ski here.

In slalom skiing, skiers race between the red and blue flags. The slalom course is in the highest village. Emma Carrick-Anderson is a British skier. She competed in the Winter Olympics.

Dallas Campbell isn't an Olympic skier. But he's ready to race.

Ski official: Left course ready, right course ready, and go!

Narrator: In an Olympic race, the difference between first and tenth place is often less than one second.

We're going to see how to prepare skis to make them go as fast as possible in the snow.

First, they "grind" the bottom of the skis to make them smooth.

Next, they use a special wax to fill in the holes. Then, they make the skis smooth again.

Now his skis are prepared, and Dallas is ready to race Emma again.

Ski official: Yeah, go.

Dallas Campbell: Ah-ha. Ah.

UNIT 6

 Amazon's Fulfillment Center

Narrator: Today Amazon is the world's largest online store. But its first warehouse was a small basement in Seattle, Washington.

Now, with more than 100 million items for sale on its website, Amazon has many large warehouses around the world called "fulfillment centers." How do they find your item? Only the central computer knows where everything is. Any item can be on any shelf.

In fact, their location is random so that workers don't take the wrong item.

After you order and pay for an item online, an Amazon worker walks through the warehouse and finds your kitchen item or your cute toy.

The computer then tells the workers the right size of the box.

Finally, your name and address goes on the box before it leaves the fulfillment center.

UNIT 7

▶ The 101-Year-Old Weather Volunteer

Reporter: Across the country, 8,500 volunteer observers record the nation's weather every day, but none has been doing it longer than 101-year-old Richard Hendrickson.

Richard: Right now, it is exactly 80.

Reporter: For 84 years now, Hendrickson's been monitoring the highs and lows from the thermometer shelter in his backyard in Bridgehampton, New York. Is this pretty much the way it's always been?

Richard: Oh, yeah.

Reporter: Real simple.

Richard: Just like that. You're getting to show age a little bit here in the joints.

Reporter: We all do.

Richard: Like we all get.

Reporter: He also checks the rainfall daily. And then glances out his dining room window to check the wind.

Richard: It's clear. There's not a cloud in the sky.

Reporter: Before calling it all in on his rotary phone …

Richard: Yeah, Bridgehampton.

Reporter: … to the National Weather Service.

Richard: The sky is clear. The wind is out of the southwest.

Reporter: When Hendrickson started recording the weather in 1930, at age 18, Herbert Hoover was president.

This is your journal from the '30s.

Richard: Sure I remember this thing. I'll be damned. In 1933. January. Clear and warm.

Reporter: Weather was important to you because you were a farmer.

Richard: Because I was a livestock farmer.

Reporter: This weekend, the National Weather Service will honor his eight decades as an observer.

Richard: Am I what? Excited? Oh, yeah, sure. I can hardly talk.

Reporter: He does it for his country, Richard Hendrickson says. Collecting the statistics that to this 101-year-old farmer are still just the facts of life.

UNIT 8

▶ Going to the International Space Station

Narrator: Most people drive or take a bus, train, or subway to work.

But Sunita Williams is different.

Every morning she gets up, takes her dog for a walk, and gets ready for work. But sometimes when she goes to work, her vehicle is very unusual. Yes, it takes her 15–20 minutes with traffic to drive her car two miles to the office in Houston, Texas.

But we're not talking about that vehicle or that office. She has a special vehicle she takes to a different office, and traffic's not a problem.

Captain Sunita Williams is an American astronaut. In 2012 she spent four months in a very special office— the International Space Station.

She traveled to the space station in this Russian Soyuz rocket.

The trip was 250 miles, straight up.

The trip to space took just nine minutes.

That's half the time it usually takes Sunita to drive to work.

Sunita Williams traveled in a tiny capsule on top of hundreds of tons of rocket power.

After she, Russian cosmonaut Yuri Malenchenko, and Japanese astronaut Akihiko Hoshide climbed the stairs and rode the elevator to the top, they went inside. Then it was time to blast off for the International Space Station.

Man: T-minus ten, nine, eight, seven, six, five, four, three, two, one.

Lift off. Lift off of the Soyuz TMA05M, carrying Suni Williams, Yuri Malenchenko, and Aki Hoshide on a journey to the International Space Station.

Name: _____ Date: _____

PART A KEY SKILLS
SCANNING FOR NUMBERS

1 Find and circle all the numbers in the article. Then complete the sentences with the correct numbers from the article.

1 Istanbul's population is about _____ people.
2 Istanbul was first called Constantinople in the year _____ .
3 The city's name was changed to Istanbul in the year _____ .
4 The Bosporus is _____ miles wide.
5 Istanbul's newest bridge opened in the year _____ .

Now read the article. Then answer the questions that follow.

Istanbul

1   More than 14 million people live in Istanbul, and the population grows by 1.5% every year. With a population of nearly 14 million people, Istanbul is Turkey's biggest city. It has played an important role in history since its creation in 657 BCE. Its first name was Byzantium, but its name changed to Constantinople in 330 CE, after the Roman Emperor Constantine decided to make it his capital. In 1453, a Turkish sultan, Mehmed II, captured the city and made it the capital of his own empire. The Turks gave the city its third name, Istanbul.

2   One of Istanbul's best-known places is the Grand Bazaar, one of the world's oldest and largest covered markets. Visitors can also visit the Hagia Sophia, the city's most famous building. It was the world's largest church for more than a thousand years, and it is now an important museum. There are also many beautiful mosques in the city, including the famous Blue Mosque.

3   Istanbul sits on the Bosporus, a waterway that is 2.3 miles (3.7 kilometers) across at is widest point and that connects the Black Sea to the Mediterranean Sea. It is also the border between Europe and Asia. About two thirds of the city is on the European side, and one third is on the Asian side. Until recently, only two bridges connected the two parts of the city, with 400,000 vehicles crossing them every day. But in 2016, a new bridge was completed, so traffic jams are not as terrible as they once were. And in 2013, the first railway tunnel opened beneath the Bosporus.

4   To get away from the noise of the city, visitors can go to the Princes' Islands, about 10 miles (16 kilometers) from downtown Istanbul. The islands have wonderful seafood restaurants, beautiful buildings, and quiet streets—and there are no cars.

    Prism 1 Reading and Writing © Cambridge University Press 2017 **Photocopiable**

PART B ADDITIONAL SKILLS

2 Write *T* (true) or *F* (false) next to the statements. Correct the false statements.

_____ 1 Istanbul's population grows by 1.5% each year.

_____

_____ 2 Istanbul is the second biggest city in Turkey.

_____

_____ 3 Constantine and Mehmed II both made the city their capital.

_____

_____ 4 The Grand Bazaar is a museum.

_____

_____ 5 The Hagia Sophia used to be a church.

_____

_____ 6 There are four bridges over the Bosporus.

_____

_____ 7 The new railway tunnel will open in a couple of years.

_____

_____ 8 People cannot drive cars on the Princes' Islands.

_____

Name: _____   Date: _____

PART A KEY VOCABULARY

1 Complete the sentences with the words in the box.

| area   cheap   countryside   downtown   local   modern   population   traffic |

1   Nicolas and Tomas went to _____ Los Angeles because there are many museums and restaurants there.
2   As soon as I saw the big field full of cows, I knew I was out of the city and in the _____ .
3   With almost 5 million people, Toronto has the highest _____ of all cities in Canada.
4   The subway in Munich, Germany is very _____ . Many of the stations feel new and have colorful walls and bright lights.
5   Many stores in the U.S. are owned by large national corporations rather than _____ business people.
6   Farah decided to take the train to work because the _____ on the roads was so bad.
7   Dana found a(n) _____ apartment. It was only $200 a month!
8   Deniz works in a(n) _____ of the city near her home so that she can walk or ride her bike to work.

2 Circle the correct definitions for the words in bold.

1   The **capital** of California is Sacramento, not Los Angeles.
   a   the largest city
   b   the most important city in a country or state; where the government is
2   Restaurants in New York City are **expensive** because their rent is usually very high.
   a   always full of people
   b   costs a lot of money; not cheap
3   Good travel writers are usually **experts** on the city or country they are writing about.
   a   someone who has a lot of skill in or a lot of knowledge about something
   b   someone who knows how to do a lot of different things
4   The children learned about different animals at the zoo. They also had the **opportunity** to pet some of the animals.
   a   enough money to do something fun
   b   a chance to do or experience something good

5   Ho Chi Minh City, Vietnam can be very **noisy** because there's a lot of traffic, and a lot of people ride motorcycles there.
   a   loud; makes a lot of noise
   b   easy to get around
6   Even though I stayed in a busy part of the city, it was **quiet** at night and I slept very well.
   a   makes little or no noise
   b   too dark to see anything
7   People in the city often got sick because the **pollution** there was bad.
   a   illness that spreads from person to person
   b   damage caused to water, air, and land by harmful materials or waste

PART B LANGUAGE DEVELOPMENT
NOUNS, VERBS, AND ADJECTIVES

3 Circle the correct part of speech for each word.

1 cheap   *noun / verb / adjective*
2 modern   *noun / verb / adjective*
3 make   *noun / verb / adjective*
4 ugly   *noun / verb / adjective*
5 village   *noun / verb / adjective*
6 expensive *noun / verb / adjective*
7 different   *noun / verb / adjective*
8 museum   *noun / verb / adjective*
9 noisy   *noun / verb / adjective*
10 traffic   *noun / verb / adjective*

ADJECTIVES

4 Underline the mistakes in the sentences. Write the correct adjectives next to the sentences.

1 There are many expensives shops and hotels in the downtown area. _____
2 They live in a beauty village in the mountains. _____
3 The people still have a very tradition way of life. _____
4 I don't like cities noisy—I prefer the countryside because it's very quiet. _____
5 The city is very pollution because there are too many cars. _____

UNIT 1 WRITING QUIZ

Name: _____   Date: _____

PART A GRAMMAR FOR WRITING
SIMPLE SENTENCES

1 Put the words in order to make simple sentences.

1 lives / My sister / small town / in a / .

_____

2 a subway / doesn't / The city / have / .

_____

3 the downtown area / People / shop in / .

_____

4 are / tall / The buildings / very / .

_____

5 every day / Alex / to work / drives / .

_____

THERE IS / THERE ARE

2 Circle the correct word to complete the sentences.

1 There *is / are* many people in the city.
2 There *is / are* 15 million tourists here every day.
3 There *isn't / aren't* many shopping malls in the downtown area.
4 There *is / are* a new movie theater in my town.
5 There *is / are* a luxury hotel at the airport.

PART B WRITING TASK

> Describe a city or town you have visited. Write about its positives and negatives.

3 Write about a city or town you have visited. Write three sentences about positive things and three sentences about negative things. Think about:

- buildings
- museums
- pollution
- parks
- restaurants
- traffic

Name: _____ Date: _____

PART A KEY SKILLS
PREVIEWING A TEXT

1 Look at the photos, title, and subtitles in the article. Answer the questions.

1 What is the article about?
  a festivals around the world
  b festivals in one country
  c the importance of festivals
2 How many festivals are described in the article?
  a two
  b three
  c four

3 Circle all of the places that are mentioned in the article.
  a Buñol
  b Florida
  c Switzerland
  d Thailand
  e the Alps

Now read the article. Then answer the questions that follow.

Local Festivals Around the World
Rattlesnake Festival

1   For the last 50 years, the small town of San Antonio, Florida has had a Rattlesnake Festival every fall. People can listen to talks about rattlesnakes and see live snakes up close in a rattlesnake show. There is live music, arts and crafts, games for children, and talks about local history, so there is something for the whole family. A highlight of the festival is a five-mile (eight-kilometer) footrace known as the Rattlesnake Run.

Tomatina Festival

2   Thousands of people from all over the world come to the small town of Buñol in Spain to take part in the Tomatina Festival, the world's biggest food fight. At 11:00 a.m. on the last Wednesday in August, trucks drive into the town square with 150,000 tomatoes. The people then spend the next hour throwing the tomatoes at each other. When the fight ends at twelve o'clock, the whole town and everyone in it is completely covered in tomatoes. Just don't wear your best clothes!

Almabtrieb Festival

3   Every year from September to October, cow herders bring their cows from high in the mountains of the Alps in Europe to the valleys for the winter. This journey is the beginning of the Almabtrieb Festival. The cows wear colorful costumes. When the cows arrive in the towns and villages, the people celebrate with delicious local food and live music.

Songkran Festival

4   The Songkran festival in Thailand is the world's biggest water fight. People celebrate the beginning of the New Year in April by throwing water at each other. So if you try to walk down the street, watch out for people with water balloons and hose pipes. You'll get very wet, but it's not a problem; April in Thailand is very hot and dry, so Songkran is a nice way to cool down. The best place to celebrate Songkran is the city of Chang Mai, where the fun continues for six days.

PART B ADDITIONAL SKILLS

2 Write *T* (true) or *F* (false) next to the statements. Correct the false statements.

_____ 1 There is live music at the Rattlesnake Festival.

_____

_____ 2 People can see photos of snakes at the Rattlesnake Festival.

_____

_____ 3 There is a five-mile bike race at the Rattlesnake Festival.

_____

_____ 4 The Tomatina Festival is in August.

_____

_____ 5 People throw tomatoes for two hours.

_____

_____ 6 It is a good idea not to wear nice clothes to the Tomatina Festival.

_____

_____ 7 The cows travel from the valleys to the mountains for the Almabtrieb festival.

_____

_____ 8 The Almabtrieb Festival starts in September.

_____

_____ 9 The Songkran Festival is a celebration of the New Year.

_____

_____ 10 April is a hot month in Thailand.

_____

UNIT 2 LANGUAGE QUIZ

Name: _____   Date: _____

PART A KEY VOCABULARY

1 Complete the sentences with the correct form of the words in the box.

celebrate   culture   highlight   history   the ground   visitor

1 Canadians _____ Canada Day on July 1 with parades and fireworks.
2 The United States is a young country. Its _____ is much shorter than countries like Egypt.
3 Hundreds of thousands of _____ from around the world attend the Berlin Film Festival every February.
4 There were no chairs at the outdoor music festival, so everyone brought blankets and sat on _____ .
5 Learning about new holidays is a good way to understand a(n) _____ that you don't know much about.
6 Fireworks are usually the _____ of Independence Day in the U.S. Everyone loves to see them.

2 Match the sentence halves.

1 Kanako got a lot of nice **gifts** _____
2 Fifteen is a **lucky** _____
3 Raquel and Yasmin are going to **take part in** _____
4 Vietnamese women wear a **traditional** _____
5 There were many **activities** _____
6 The Snow and Ice Festival is **popular** _____

a dress called "Ao Dai."
b every winter in China.
c the Halloween parade.
d number for some Spanish people.
e for her birthday from her friends.
f for children at the party.

PART B LANGUAGE DEVELOPMENT
PREPOSITIONS OF TIME AND PLACE

3 Complete the paragraph with *in*, *on*, or *at*.

> New Year's Eve celebrations in many countries around the world start (1)_____ the evening (2)_____ December 31 and finish early (3)_____ the morning (4)_____ New Year's Day, January 1. People often have parties with friends and relatives in their homes, and then they go outside (5)_____ about 11:45 p.m. to wait for the fireworks. (6)_____ London, the New Year officially starts when Big Ben strikes midnight. (7)_____ Scotland, people celebrate the New Year with a celebration called Hogmanay. (8)_____ New York, there is a giant ball at the top of a tower in Times Square. (9)_____ one minute to midnight, the ball starts coming down the tower, and (10)_____ exactly midnight, people celebrate with music and fireworks. Most people stay (11)_____ home on New Year's Day because they are too tired to go out after such a late night.

ADVERBS OF FREQUENCY

4 Rewrite the sentences with the correct adverbs of frequency in the box. Use the words in parentheses to help you.

| always   never   often   sometimes   usually |

1 We go to Rio de Janeiro for Carnival. (every year)

_____

2 I spend my birthday with my family. (almost every year)

_____

3 The Chinese New Year starts in January. (some years)

_____

4 We go to parties. (at no time)

_____

5 At the festival, people exchange gifts with friends and relatives. (common)

_____

Prism 1 Reading and Writing © Cambridge University Press 2017 **Photocopiable**

UNIT 2 WRITING QUIZ

Name: _____ Date: _____

PART A GRAMMAR FOR WRITING
SIMPLE SENTENCES

1 Correct the error in each sentence. Rewrite the complete sentences.

1 We eat food traditional.

_____

2 My mother a new dress wears.

_____

3 Starts the music at midnight.

_____

4 I gives my sister a gift.

_____

5 My family for three days celebrates.

_____

2 Underline the objects in the sentences and circle the prepositional phrases.

1 People celebrate the festival of Diwali in India.
2 Everyone wears new clothes on the third day.
3 People light small lanterns in their houses.
4 They draw flowers on the ground.
5 People give gifts to their loved ones.

PART B WRITING TASK

Describe a festival or special event that you celebrate with your family.

3 Write a paragraph about the festival or special event. Include a topic sentence, at least four supporting sentences, and a concluding sentence.

Name: _____   Date: _____

Read the article. Then answer the questions that follow.

1   An encyclopedia is a book or a set of books with information about almost any kind of subject you have an interest in. The subjects in encyclopedias are listed alphabetically to make them easy to find. The *Encyclopaedia Britannica* is the oldest English language encyclopedia in the world. It has articles by over 4,000 writers on more than 32,000 pages. There are 32 volumes, and it weighs 129 pounds (58 kilograms). In 2010, after 244 years, the last volumes were printed, and *Encyclopaedia Britannica* became a digital encyclopedia only. The world of encyclopedias began to change in 1993, when Microsoft, the world's largest computer software company, launched its own encyclopedia, *Encarta*. Microsoft had enough money to pay a large team of professional writers and programmers. Customers paid a lot of money to buy it on CDs or online. But after only eight years, the world changed again.

2   *Wikipedia* was launched in January 2001 by Jimmy Wales and Larry Sanger. They did not pay for teams of writers—they simply waited for people to write for fun. They also did not pay people to check what others were writing—again, everyone worked for free. In addition, customers did not buy their encyclopedias as books or CDs—it was all free on the Internet. Nobody thought that *Wikipedia* could compete with the other encyclopedias, but it is now one of the largest and most popular encyclopedias in the world.

3   Of course, there were problems, especially in the beginning. People sometimes wrote about subjects that they did not really understand, and they did not always have all the correct information. Some writers had very strong feelings about a subject, so readers were not sure if they were reading opinions or facts. Sometimes people invented facts or gave false information, which made the people they wrote about angry.

4   Fortunately, things improved, and problems like these are not as common as they were. Recent studies have shown that false information on *Wikipedia* is usually quickly corrected. There are only a few mistakes in most online encyclopedias, and there are now good systems to find and fix problems quickly. It is still a good idea to check your facts somewhere else too, but it looks like *Wikipedia* is here to stay, at least until the next big change in the world of encyclopedias comes along.

PART A KEY SKILLS
READING FOR MAIN IDEAS

1 Circle the best answers.

1 What is the main idea of paragraph 1?
   a The history of encyclopedias
   b the heaviest encyclopedia in the world
2 what is the main idea of paragraph 2?
   a a new encyclopedia on CDs
   b a new encyclopedia online
3 What is the main idea of paragraph 3?
   a opinions about Wikipedia
   b problems with Wikipedia
4 What is the main idea of paragraph 4?
   a improvements to Wikipedia
   b mistakes in Wikipedia
5 What is the best title for the article?
   a How Wikipedia Changed the World of Encyclopedias
   b How to Use an Encyclopedia

MAKING INFERENCES

2 Choose the best answer.

1 What can you infer about *Encyclopaedia Britannica*?
   a There were a lot of mistakes in the printed volumes.
   b The company does not make encyclopedias anymore.
   c In the 1990s, fewer people used print encyclopedias than in the past.
2 Why do people write for *Wikipedia*?
   a They get a lot of money for writing.
   b They don't like other encyclopedias.
   c They enjoy writing and they want to help.
3 Why was *Wikipedia* successful?
   a *Encarta* had technical problems.
   b *Wikipedia* was free.
   c *Wikipedia* writers sometimes invented facts.
4 Why did some people get angry about *Wikipedia* articles?
   a The writers had strong feelings.
   b The articles were not interesting.
   c The information was not always true.
5 Why does the writer recommend checking your facts somewhere else?
   a Encyclopedias on the Internet sometimes have mistakes.
   b People do not usually fix problems.
   c You can trust books more than online encyclopedias.

Name: _____ Date: _____

PART A KEY VOCABULARY

1 Complete the sentences with the correct form of the words in the box.

| affect collect educational free interest security software |

1 I don't usually spend money on new computer programs because there are so many available for _____ .
2 Spending too much time on the Internet can _____ your social skills. After a while, it might become difficult to speak to people face-to-face.
3 Una has always had a(n) _____ in computer engineering, so she is planning to major in it in college.
4 Chang only lets his children use a tablet to watch _____ videos. They can't use it to play games.
5 My new computer _____ will help me manage my money.
6 Mariana changes her computer password every week. She feels better knowing she takes steps for extra _____ .
7 Some organizations _____ old computers and tablets from people, which they repair and donate to schools.

2 Circle the correct definitions for the words in bold.

1 You should **record** your teacher's lecture so you can listen to it outside of class.
   a to store sounds, pictures, or information on a camera or computer so that they can be used in the future
   b to pay attention to something you see or hear very carefully
2 One **benefit** of smartphones in the classroom is that students can use them to look up new vocabulary words.
   a a reason why something is bad
   b a good or helpful result or effect
3 Meryem is a **creative** teacher. She always finds new and interesting ways to use technology with her students.
   a good at thinking of new ideas or creating new and unusual things
   b good at learning new facts and memorizing things you read
4 Akihiro **downloads** new music almost every day. He has thousands of songs on his computer.
   a shops for things online
   b copies computer programs, music, or other information electronically from the Internet to a computer
5 My grades began to **improve** when I stopped playing so many video games. My parents and teachers were very pleased.
   a to change in a negative way
   b to get better or to make something better
6 The company plans to reveal its **secret** design for a new robot next week.
   a not known or seen by other people
   b something that people probably won't like
7 Amanda has a wonderful **imagination**. She can read a story and then draw the people from the story on her computer.
   a the part of your mind that creates ideas or pictures of things that are not real or that you have not seen
   b the part of your mind that makes you understand the things you read

PART B LANGUAGE DEVELOPMENT
COMPOUND NOUNS

3 Use one word from each box to complete the sentences with compound nouns. In some items, more than one answer may be possible.

computer email key smart video Web	address board game page phone program

1 She spends all her time on the Internet playing her favorite _____ .
2 I need your _____ to send you the file.
3 I usually text and send emails from my _____ because I always have it with me.
4 The _____ is broken on my computer so I can't type the letter *M*.
5 A(n) _____ is a set of instructions that makes a computer do something.
6 I read a lot of information about the company's history on its _____ .

GIVING OPINIONS

4 Read the sentences. Find the mistakes in the underlined words. Then rewrite the sentences correctly.

1 <u>I am thinking that</u> online shopping is usually safe.

_____

2 <u>It's seem to me that</u> social media is very popular.

_____

3 <u>In my opinion that</u> some video games aren't suitable for children.

_____

4 <u>I think, that</u> the Internet has made life easier.

_____

5 <u>I believe it</u> Internet banking is better than traditional banking.

_____

Name: _____   Date: _____

PART A GRAMMAR FOR WRITING
CONNECTING IDEAS

1 Join the pairs of sentences to make one compound sentence using the word in parentheses.

1 I have an email account. I don't use it now. (but)

_____

2 I use the Internet. I have two email accounts. (and)

_____

3 My friends shop online a lot. I like shopping at regular stores. (but)

_____

4 Some video games are fun to play. They can teach children about math. (and)

_____

5 Social media is very popular. It hasn't replaced traditional media. (but)

_____

2 Rewrite the sentence pairs. For each pair, use the word in parentheses to connect the idea in the second sentence to the idea in the first sentence.

1 I buy films online. I upload my own films. (also)

_____

2 You can read news articles on this website. You can read people's comments. (too)

_____

3 The Internet has many advantages. It also has some disadvantages. (however)

_____

4 I have a bank account online. I shop online a lot. (too)

_____

5 I buy books on the Internet. You can buy videos on the Internet. (also)

_____

PART B WRITING TASK

Social media has changed the way we read the news. Do you agree or disagree?

3 Write a paragraph about your opinion on the topic. Include a topic sentence with a controlling idea, three supporting ideas, and a concluding sentence.

Name: _____ Date: _____

PART A KEY SKILLS
USING YOUR KNOWLEDGE TO PREDICT CONTENT

1 Put a check next to five things that tell you that it is going to rain soon. Then read the article and check your answers.

1 There are many birds flying high in the sky. ☐
2 Cows in the field are lying down close to one another. ☐
3 There is a strong smell of flowers. ☐
4 There are low, dark clouds. ☐
5 There are no clouds in the morning sky. ☐
6 There are low clouds on a winter evening. ☐
7 The sky is red in the evening. ☐
8 The sky is red in the morning. ☐
9 The moon is very clear. ☐
10 The grass is wet in the morning. ☐

Now read the article. Then answer the questions that follow.

Predicting the Weather

1 If we want to know what the weather will be like tomorrow, we check the TV, Internet, or a weather app. Modern weather forecasting is done with satellites, airplanes, computers, ships, and balloons. Can we also predict the weather ourselves? Here are some older ways that may help you predict the weather. But remember—they are not scientific.

2 • Watch animals and plants. If birds are flying high in the sky, they think the weather is going to be good. If they are all on the ground or low in the trees, a storm may be coming. Cows also usually lie down close together before a rain storm. You can even smell the weather sometimes: a strong plant smell in the air means the plants are getting ready for rain. Flowers also smell better before it rains.

3 • If there are low, dark clouds covering the sky, it is going to rain soon. Long, thin clouds high in the sky can also mean that it will rain tomorrow or the next day but probably not today. Also, if clouds are moving in different directions, bad weather can be expected. But clouds do not always mean bad news: in winter, a cloudy evening means the next morning will be warmer.

4 • Sometimes the wind predicts what weather to expect. In many places, wind from the east brings rain storms, while wind from the west brings good weather.

5 • Sometimes the sky looks red because it is dry. If the sky is red in the evening, it means the dry air is in the west, and we can expect dry weather. If the sky is red in the morning, the dry air is in the east, and wet weather is coming. However, in some places, weather moves from east to west, so a red sky has the opposite meaning. You can also predict the weather by looking at the moon. If the moon is beautiful and clear, the clear weather will not last, and it will probably rain soon.

6 • One last thing: look out for wet grass in the morning. This usually means a dry day. Of course, it might also simply mean that it rained last night!

READING FOR DETAILS

2 Choose the correct detail to complete each sentence.

1 Modern weather forecasting uses *balloons / birds* to predict the weather.
2 Animals such as *cows / sheep* can help predict the weather.
3 Flowers smell *better / worse* before it rains.
4 Wind from the *east / west* often brings rain.
5 *A red sky / wet grass* in the morning usually means dry weather.

PART B ADDITIONAL SKILLS

3 Circle the correct answer to the questions.

1 Where do you think you would see this article?
   a a science textbook
   b an advertisement
   c a blog
2 What can you infer about the information in paragraph 2?
   a The behavior of animals is unpredictable.
   b Some animals know when rain is coming.
   c No one knows why cows lie down close together.
3 What is the main idea of paragraph 3?
   a The clouds can help you predict the weather.
   b It might rain if the ground is wet.
   c You can learn about the weather from plants and animals.
4 What is the main idea of paragraph 5?
   a The sky can help you predict the weather.
   b Heavy wind means rain is coming.
   c A beautiful sky may be bad news.
5 What is probably true about the suggestions in the text?
   a They are better than scientific methods.
   b They won't always be correct.
   c Only animals can predict the weather.

Name: _____   Date: _____

PART A KEY VOCABULARY

1 Match the sentence halves.

1 The earthquake damaged _____	a which turned the rain to ice.
2 I can't **decide** if _____	b everyone at the beach went home.
3 The deep snow **covered** _____	c **almost** every building in the city.
4 The temperature **dropped** suddenly, _____	d I want to go skiing or ice skating today.
5 The cold weather is expected to **last** _____	e the city in white.
6 When the **lightning** started, _____	f it caused floods in three states.
7 The storm was **huge**; _____	g for two more weeks.

2 Complete the sentences with the words from the box.

> careful   dangerous   precipitation   rise   shock   thunder

1 The amount of _____ was very low last year so none of the farmers' crops grew well.

2 Be _____ when you drive home tonight. The heavy rain is making it difficult to see the road.

3 It's cold outside now, but the temperature is expected to _____ by noon.

4 When Ana went outside without her sweater, the icy, cold wind was quite a _____ .

5 It's _____ to be outside for too long in hot weather, especially if you don't drink enough water.

6 It was a quiet day at the park until suddenly the sound of _____ scared everyone.

PART B LANGUAGE DEVELOPMENT
COLLOCATIONS WITH TEMPERATURE
DESCRIBING A GRAPH

3 Look at the graph. Complete the description with the words from the box.

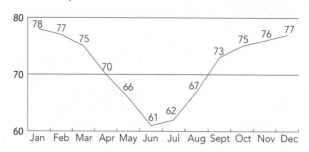

| decrease | falls | high | increase | low | maximum | minimum | reaches | rises | drops |

The graph shows the average daytime temperature in Johannesburg, South Africa over a year. As you can see, we have (1) _____ temperatures in December and January (our summer), and (2) _____ temperatures in June and July (our winter). After the winter, the temperature (3) _____ to 67° F in August, and then there's a(n) (4) _____ to 75° F in October. The temperature (5) _____ 77° F in December, and then goes up to a(n) (6) _____ temperature of 78° F in January. After that, the temperature (7) _____ to 75° F in March, and then there's a(n) (8) _____ to 66° F in May. The (9) _____ temperature is in June when it (10) _____ to 61° F.

Prism 1 Reading and Writing © Cambridge University Press 2017 **Photocopiable**

Name: _____ Date: _____

PART A GRAMMAR FOR WRITING
COMPARATIVE AND SUPERLATIVE ADJECTIVES

1 Complete the sentences with the correct form of the adjectives in parentheses.

1 The _____ place on earth is Death Valley in the United States. (hot)
2 Temperatures are usually _____ in summer than in spring. (high)
3 This week is much _____ than last week. (sunny)
4 The _____ tornado in history was in Bangladesh in 1989. (dangerous)
5 The _____ temperature ever recorded was –129° F (–89.2 °C), in Antarctica. (low)
6 This summer is _____ than last summer. (dry)
7 The _____ place in the world is Mawsynram in India. (rainy)
8 I think the weather is getting _____ every year. (extreme)
9 The Sahara Desert is the _____ desert in the world. (big)
10 If you're stuck in the desert, stay in your car—you'll be _____ to see than if you get out. (easy)

PART B WRITING TASK

Describe the weather in San Francisco, California.

2 Write a paragraph about the climate in San Francisco, California. Use the Internet or a weather app to find information about the average temperature and average monthly precipitation in the city. Choose two interesting facts about temperature and two interesting facts about precipitation, and write sentences about them. Use data to support your statements.

Name: _____   Date: _____

PART A KEY SKILLS
SCANNING TO PREDICT CONTENT

1   Read the statements and scan the article. Write *T* (true) or *F* (false) next to the statements.

_____   1   Endurance riding is a fast growing sport.
_____   2   The health of the horses must be checked during the ride.
_____   3   There is a maximum age for endurance riders.
_____   4   Some people use camels in endurance riding.
_____   5   Endurance riding is now an Olympic sport.

Now read the article. Then answer the questions that follow.

Endurance Riding

1   The sport of endurance riding, where horse riders race over a long distance, is one of the world's fastest growing sports. There are now around 800 international events every year. The rules are different in various countries, but a typical race is around 100 miles (160 kilometers), which can take between ten and twelve hours to complete.

2   The most important rule is that the horses must be safe. For this reason, vets check their health regularly during the race, and the horses always have time to eat, rest, and drink water. The riders also need to think carefully about their horse's health because if the vets think a horse can't continue safely, it has to stop. The winner is the first healthy horse to finish—a horse that is sick or too tired cannot win the race. Teams are also expected to be kind to their horses after they are too old to race.

3   Endurance riding started in the United States as a test for horses in the military. In order to pass the test, the horses had to carry 200 pounds (91 kilograms) and walk for 300 miles (482 kilometers). The walk usually took five days. In the 1950s, endurance riding became a competitive sport. It is unique because people of all ages can take part in it—there is no minimum or maximum age for participants. Families can ride together, yet still compete individually.

4   Endurance riding became popular internationally after it reached the United Arab Emirates (UAE). The first endurance event in the UAE was in 1993, when camels as well as horses raced through the desert for over 25 miles (40 kilometers). Since then the link between endurance riding and the UAE has grown stronger: the World Championships took place there in 1998, and the UAE now wants to have the sport included in the Olympic Games.

PART B ADDITIONAL SKILLS

2 Choose the correct answer.

1 *Endurance* means _____ .
   a the ability to remember lots of information
   b the ability to go very fast
   c the ability to go a long way

2 Endurance riding started _____ .
   a in the United States
   b in the UAE
   c in the Olympics

3 *Vets* are _____ .
   a doctors for animals
   b people who watch a race
   c horses in a race

4 In endurance riding, horses must be _____ .
   a large
   b smart
   c healthy

5 A *link* is _____ .
   a something that horse riders wear
   b a connection between two things
   c a type of competition between two countries

Name: _____   Date: _____

PART A KEY VOCABULARY

1 Complete the sentences with the correct form of the words in the box.

| accident   ancient   challenging   course   in shape   swimming   take place |

1 Many _____ sports that began thousands of years ago, like running, wrestling, and horse riding, are still popular today.
2 Even if the weather is bad, the marathon will still _____ on Saturday morning at 7:00 a.m.
3 It was _____ for Adrienne to bike across the country by herself, but she felt great when she finished.
4 My grandfather walks several miles every day in order to stay _____ .
5 _____ is Mie's favorite sport. She goes to the pool every morning before school.
6 The _____ for the bike race was difficult because it included a lot of hills.
7 The heavy wind caused the boat to get into a(n) _____ with another boat. Fortunately, no one was hurt.

2 Circle the correct definitions for the words in bold.

1 The top prize for the dance **competition** was $1,000.
   a an organized event in which people help each other
   b an organized event in which people try to win a prize by being the best
2 **Throw** the baseball to me, and I will catch it.
   a to send something through the air, kicking it with your foot
   b to send something through the air, pushing it out of your hand
3 Victor goes hiking every day because he wants to **climb** Mount Kilimanjaro next year.
   a to go up something or onto the top of something
   b to walk through a park or a forest on flat land
4 There are some **strange** sports around the world, such as bed racing, pie eating, and dog surfing.
   a something fun that you want to take part in
   b not familiar; difficult to understand; different
5 At age 13, Franco was the youngest **participant** in the race.
   a someone who takes part in an activity
   b someone who organizes an activity
6 The two best teams will **compete** against each other for the world championship.
   a to take part in a race or competition; to try to be more successful than someone else
   b to train your body or mind to be ready for a competition

PART B LANGUAGE DEVELOPMENT
PREPOSITIONS OF MOVEMENT

3 Circle the correct prepositions to complete the email.

Hi Anna,

I'm happy that you're coming to my house next week, but it's difficult to find it. You should take bus number 44 to the City Museum. When you get off the bus, go ⁽¹⁾ *across / past / under* the road. You'll see the museum in front of you. Go ⁽²⁾ *over / past / through* the museum, and stop when you get to the park. Go ⁽³⁾ *around / over / through* the park. You'll go ⁽⁴⁾ *around / through / under* the lake in the middle of the park and then ⁽⁵⁾ *along / over / past* the little bridge. The street on the other side of the park is my street, and my house is number 17. Good luck!

Maria

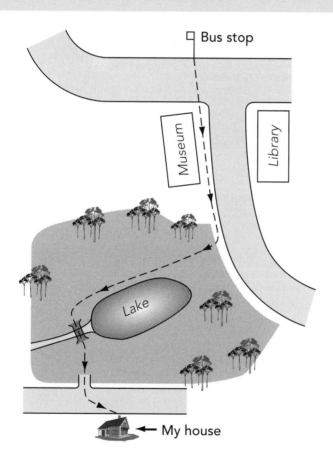

Name: _____ Date: _____

PART A GRAMMAR FOR WRITING
SUBJECT AND VERB AGREEMENT

1 Circle the correct words to complete the sentences.

1 My *brother / brothers* plays football.
2 The player *throw / throws* the ball as far as she can.
3 My friends and I *watch / watches* a lot of sports on TV.
4 The best *player / players* on the team win a trophy.
5 She *run / runs* very fast.

2 Write the correct form of the verb in parentheses to complete the sentences.

1 The horses _____ to drink a lot. (need)
2 We _____ the ball with our gloves. (catch)
3 Basketball and football _____ popular sports in the United States. (be)
4 He _____ TV every night. (watch)
5 The girls on the baseball team _____ to practice every evening. (try)

PART B WRITING TASK

Write about a race or other competition.

3 Write a paragraph about a race or other competition. Write general information about the competition in the topic sentence. Write supporting sentences about the events in the competition in the correct order. Use transition words to show the time order.

Name: _____   Date: _____

Read the article. Then answer the questions that follow.

The Tata Group

1   The Tata Group is one of India's best-known companies. It employs more than half a million people worldwide. It is rich and successful, and has an excellent reputation for doing good things and treating people well. For example, a recent survey found that it was the world's 11th most reputable company. It also gives a lot of money to good causes, such as projects to bring clean water to poor families and to teach children how to read and write.

2   The company was founded in 1868 by Jamsetji Tata, an Indian businessman. He created many businesses, including the first hotel in India with electricity. These days he is known as the "Father of Indian Industry." The city of Jamshedpur, where Tata's first iron and steel factory was built in 1912, gets its name from Jamsetji Tata. Today Jamshedpur is still an important center for Tata companies, including Tata Steel and Tata Motors.

3   In 2000, the business expanded and started buying other companies around the world. The first one was Tetley, a large British tea company. Later, Tata bought some other famous British companies, like the carmaker Jaguar Land Rover. In 2007, when Tata bought its most expensive company, Corus, for $12 billion, Tata Steel became one of the world's biggest steel companies.

4   However, not everything with the Tata name is big and expensive. The Tata Nano was introduced in 2009 and is the world's cheapest car. It is a tiny car, which makes it good for India's crowded cities. The original price was 1 lakh rupees, or about $1,500, but the price has gone up a little since then. The Nano is a symbol of Tata's main goals: to make life better for poor people, and to show the world that Indian technology and business are as good as anything in the rich world.

PART A KEY SKILLS
WORKING OUT MEANING FROM CONTEXT

1 Find the words in bold in the text. Then complete the statements.

1   If you have a good **reputation**, _____ .
   a   people like and trust you
   b   you can make a lot of money

2   A **survey** is _____ .
   a   a place where many people work to make things
   b   an examination of people's opinions by asking different people the same questions

3   If you help a good **cause**, _____ .
   a   you try to make the world a better place for other people, not just for yourself
   b   you help other people because you want them to help you later

4   **Iron** and **steel** are _____ .
   a   kinds of plastic used to make cups and water bottles
   b   types of metal used to make machines and cars

5   A **lakh** _____ .
   a   is a name for a big number in India, Pakistan, Bangladesh, and Sri Lanka
   b   is a type of car used in Delhi and other large Indian cities

ANNOTATING A TEXT

2 Annotate the article you read. Highlight important names, dates, numbers, and ideas. Use your notes to answer the questions.

1 When was the Tata Group founded?
   a 2007
   b 2000
   c 1868
2 What did the Tata Group do in 1912?
   a It started a tea company.
   b It bought Corus.
   c It built an iron and steel factory.
3 Who or what is the city of Jamshedpur named after?
   a the founder of the Tata Group
   b the world's cheapest car
   c a famous British company
4 Which company did the Tata Group's buy first?
   a Tetley
   b Corus
   c Jaguar Land Rover
5 How much did the original Tata Nano cost?
   a $1,500
   b $2,000
   c $1,200

PART B ADDITIONAL SKILLS

3 Write *T* (true) or *F* (false) next to the statements. Correct the false statements.

1 _____ The Tata Group treats people in India badly.

_____

2 _____ Before the Tata Group was founded, hotels in India did not have electricity.

_____

3 _____ The most expensive company bought by the Tata Group is Jaguar Land Rover.

_____

4 _____ Only rich people can afford to buy the Tata Nano.

_____

5 _____ The Tata Nano is easy to drive in crowded cities.

_____

Name: _____ Date: _____

PART A KEY VOCABULARY

1 Complete the sentences with the correct form of the words in the box.

advertise colleague customer occupation partner result run

1 Nathan was nervous because he was waiting for the _____ of his final exam.
2 Francine always knew that her _____ would be in the arts. She loved singing and dancing from a young age.
3 The best place for a company to _____ its products is on social media.
4 Luisa's dream is to move to Costa Rica and _____ a small café near the beach.
5 Erdem and Gul met while they were _____ at a software company. A year later, they got married.
6 Sang wanted to open a restaurant, but he needed a(n) _____ to help him manage and pay for it.
7 During her first year in business, Sofia focused on making her _____ happy so that they would return in the future.

2 Match the sentence halves.

1 All of the top managers have _____
2 Larisa is **applying** for _____
3 The tech company **introduced** _____
4 Hana **organized** _____
5 You don't need a lot of money to **set up** _____
6 Liu's **goal** is to make _____
7 The new steel company will **employ** _____

a a scholarship to help her pay for college.
b hundreds of people from the area.
c a company if you have a computer.
d $1 million before the age of 30.
e **offices** on the 25th floor.
f a meeting with everyone in her company.
g its new computer to the public today.

PART B LANGUAGE DEVELOPMENT
COLLOCATIONS WITH BUSINESS

3 Complete the sentences with one or two words.

1 We are still a small company, but we plan to e _ _ _ _ _ our business over the next year.
2 If you want the bank to give your company money, you need to show them a very good business p _ _ _.
3 Many people try to s _ _ _ _ a new business, but only a few succeed.
4 My brother is my business p _ _ _ _ _ _. We run the company together.
5 We have a business c_ _ _ _ _ _ in China who understands the market and can help increase our sales.

BUSINESS VOCABULARY

4 Put the words in order to make sentences.

1 my office / with / I share / two / other people / .

_____

2 run better / helped / The new / my computer / software / .

_____

3 asked / The employee / for / his boss / a day off / .

_____

4 for quality / must be / A new product / tested / .

_____

5 more than / employs / 500 / The mall / people / .

_____

Name: _____   Date: _____

PART A GRAMMAR FOR WRITING
THE SIMPLE PRESENT AND THE SIMPLE PAST

1 Write the correct form of the verbs in parentheses to complete the paragraph.
Use the simple past or the simple present.

> Nokia is a Finnish technology company. It (1) _____ (make) cell phones and computer software. It (2) _____ (employ) over 100,000 people in 120 countries. Nokia (3) _____ (start) in 1865. In those days, the company (4) _____ (make) paper. Later it also (5) _____ (produce) everything from boots to televisions. However, in the 1990s it (6) _____ (sell) all those other businesses. The company (7) _____ (be) very successful making cell phones from 1998 to 2012. Then people (8) _____ (start) buying their phones from other companies. Now Nokia (9) _____ (work) with Microsoft to make smartphones. Of course, their cell phones (10) _____ (be) much smaller than they were twenty years ago.

TIME CLAUSES WITH *WHEN*

2 Rewrite the sentences using *when.*

1 The partners had enough money. They set up their business.

_____

2 The employee quit his job. He found a job a job that paid more money.

_____

3 The company's product failed. They introduced a new product.

_____

4 The economy improved. The business made more money.

_____

5 Cell phones were invented. People could communicate more easily.

_____

PART B WRITING TASK

Write a narrative paragraph about a business person.

3 Choose a business person and do some research about his or her history in business.
Include some interesting facts and details in your paragraph.

Name: _____ Date: _____

Read the article. The answer the questions that follow.

Life Without Limbs

1   Most of us never think about our limbs—our arms and our legs. We need all four, right? And losing one limb would be a disaster. But think, for a moment, about how life would be with no limbs at all. What could you do? What couldn't you do?

2   Meet Nick Vujicic. He was born without arms or legs, but he's still one of the most positive people on Earth. He doesn't want you to feel sorry for him because he sees his situation as an opportunity, not a problem.

3   Although he doesn't have arms or legs, he does have feet and two toes. This means he has learned to do many things. He can write by holding a pen between his toes, and he can type on a computer. He can throw a ball, play drums, comb his hair, brush his teeth and answer the phone. He also plays golf, goes swimming, and has even tried skydiving. He got married in 2012.

4   He was born in Australia in 1982, and had a difficult childhood. The other children at school laughed at him because he was different, and this made him very sad and lonely. He didn't understand why he needed to be different from everyone else. Then his mother showed him a newspaper article about another disabled man who still achieved his dreams. Nick understood that he wasn't alone, and this inspired him.

5   When he was 17, he started giving speeches and presentations about his life and his positive attitude. Since then he has traveled around the world and spoken to millions of people. He now lives in California, where he is the leader of an organization called "Life Without Limbs." This incredible organization helps young people feel positive about themselves.

PART A KEY SKILLS
MAKING INFERENCES

1   Circle the correct answers. Then write the sentences from the article from which you were able to infer the answer.

1   Does Nick feel sorry for himself? *Yes / No*

_____

2   Does Nick like to challenge himself by trying new things? *Yes / No*

_____

3   Did Nick have a lot of friends when he was a child? *Yes / No*

_____

4   Did Nick's mother encourage him to follow his dreams? *Yes / No*

_____

5   Does Nick want to help other young people with disabilities? *Yes / No*

_____

PART B ADDITIONAL SKILLS

2 Circle the correct answers to make the sentences true. Only one answer in each statement is correct.

1   Nick ...
    a   lost his limbs in an accident.
    b   was born without limbs.
    c   has legs but no arms.

2   Nick's mother ...
    a   helps him comb his hair.
    b   taught him to play golf.
    c   gave him an inspiring newspaper article.

3   When Nick was a child, he ...
    a   was sad and lonely.
    b   understood why he was different.
    c   inspired other young people.

4   In paragraph 5, *attitude* means ...
    a   the things you experience in your life.
    b   the physical strength you have in your body.
    c   the way you think or feel about something.

5   "Life Without Limbs" ...
    a   sells books and videos.
    b   asks young people to give speeches.
    c   encourages young people to be positive.

Name: _____   Date: _____

PART A KEY VOCABULARY

1 Circle the correct definition of the words in bold.

1 Because the **blind** man couldn't see, he used his ears to understand the world around him.
  a not able to see
  b not able to hear
2 I plan to **achieve** my goal of getting a Ph.D. in the next four years.
  a to try very hard to reach a goal
  b to be successful at something difficult
3 Daniel works hard, but he was also born with the **talent** to become a successful singer in the future.
  a a natural ability to do something well
  b something you really want to do when you are older
4 Everyone thought Amelia was **brave** because she traveled around the world by herself.
  a not afraid of dangerous or difficult situations
  b physically strong
5 I **respect** people who are kind and helpful to others, and I see them as my role models.
  a to encourage people to help others
  b to like or to have a good opinion of someone because of their knowledge, achievements, or actions
6 Derrek's story is **incredible**. He graduated from high school when he was only 13, got his master's degree when he was 18, and started his first successful company when he was 20.
  a not surprising because it was expected
  b very difficult to believe; amazing
7 Based on several tests, Yolanda is one of the most **intelligent** students at her school.
  a able to learn and understand things easily; smart
  b able to study for long hours at a time

2 Complete the sentences with the correct form of the words in the box.

dream   former   honest   inspire   operation   take care of   train

1 Her _____ went well, so Lily will be able to leave the hospital in two days.
2 Gabriel has a new job, so he needs someone to _____ his children for a few hours after school.
3 Rachel's mother always helped others, and she _____ Rachel to become a doctor.
4 I have many more responsibilities at my new job than I had at my _____ one.
5 Sarah and Eve want to run a marathon. They started to _____ by running a few miles every day.
6 The _____ of many athletes is to compete in the Olympics.
7 Efrain's friends say he is the most _____ person they know, and they always trust his opinion.

PART B LANGUAGE DEVELOPMENT
NOUN PHRASES WITH *OF*

3 Complete the sentences with a phrase from each box.

Box A
at the top   the manager
at the end   a kind   a type

Box B
of music   of computer   of the film
of the IT department   of the building

1 We left the movie theater _____ .
2 A laptop is _____ .
3 His apartment is _____ . It has amazing views.
4 Hip-hop is _____ .
5 At his new job, he's _____ . He has twenty computer programmers working under him.

ADJECTIVES TO DESCRIBE PEOPLE

4 Read the conversations. Choose the best adjective from the box to describe person B.

difficult   intelligent   kind   patient   selfish

1 **A:** Sorry I'm so late. I missed my bus. Are you angry with me?
   B: No, of course not. I don't get angry easily. It's fine. _____
2 **A:** Can I use your pen, please?
   B: No. It's my special pen. I don't care if you don't have one. Go and buy your own pen! _____
3 **A:** Oh no, I left my money at home. I don't have enough for a sandwich!
   B: No problem, you can have my sandwich. Can I help you in any other way? _____
4 **A:** I don't understand this question. It's very difficult. I don't know where to start.
   B: Well, I can usually understand things like this. If you draw a diagram, it's much easier. I'll explain it to you.
   _____
5 **A:** Do you want to go out for dinner tonight? We can meet at that new Chinese restaurant at 8:00.
   B: Sure, I'd love to spend time with you, but I want to watch the football game first, so I'll be there at about 9:00. Oh, and I don't like Chinese food, so can we get a pizza instead? _____

UNIT 7 WRITING QUIZ

Name: _____   Date: _____

PART A GRAMMAR FOR WRITING
MODALS OF NECESSITY

1 Which of these things should role models be? Write sentences using *should, must, have to,* or *should not, must not, do not have to.* Use the phrases in parentheses.

1 (be reliable) _____

2 (be difficult) _____

3 (respect other people's opinions) _____

4 (be lazy) _____

5 (be kind) _____

PART B WRITING TASK

Who do you think is a good role model for parents? Why?

2 Write a paragraph that answers the questions. In the topic sentence, introduce the person you chose and explain why you think he or she is a good role model for parents. In the supporting sentences, write the qualities of a good role model and some examples. In the concluding sentence, restate your main idea in a different way.

Name: _____ Date: _____

Read the article. The answer the questions that follow.

Back to the Moon ... and Beyond

1   It has been over 50 years since the first man (and the last man) visited the moon. This may seem surprising: we have seen a lot of advances in technology since the 1970s. Shouldn't it be easy to visit the moon again?

2   In fact, there are some problems with manned missions, compared to sending just robots. These missions are expensive, and there are many other things for countries to spend money on. There's also the question of why we need to explore the moon again. After all, the U.S. won the race to the moon in 1969.

3   But if not the moon, what about Mars? Will we see astronauts traveling there in the next few decades? It's not as crazy as it sounds. There have already been many unmanned missions to Mars, and both NASA (the U.S. Space Agency) and ESA (the European Space Agency) say they want to send manned missions to Mars in the 2030s.

4   Evidence shows that of all the planets in the solar system, Mars is the most similar to Earth. The planet is colder than Earth, with an average surface temperature of -67° F (-55 °C), but it can be much warmer in places—up to about 95° F (35 °C)—when it is closest to the sun. It also has a lot of water, mostly in the form of ice. The atmosphere is mainly made up of carbon dioxide (CO_2), so humans would not be able to breathe there. The pressure is also much lower than on Earth, so people would need to wear special space suits. Life would not be easy for astronauts on Mars, but it would be no worse than on the moon.

5   What about the long journey? The distance between Mars and Earth changes all the time because the two planets orbit at different speeds around the sun. In fact, in 2018, the distance will be as little as 35.8 million miles (57.6 million kilometers). Most journeys to Mars have taken around six months, so a manned mission to Mars and back would probably take at least a year. That's certainly a long time, but one astronaut, Sergei Krikalev, once spent over 800 days on board the International Space Station, so perhaps the journey to Mars would not be so bad.

PART A KEY SKILLS
IDENTIFYING THE AUTHOR'S PURPOSE

1 Circle the correct answer to make each statement true.

1 The purpose of the text is to ...
   a persuade governments to go to the moon again.
   b describe the high cost of space travel.
   c explain the possibility of traveling to Mars.

2 You could find this text in ...
   a an advertisement for space tourism.
   b a magazine about space travel.
   c a fiction novel.

3 The author mentions NASA and the ESA in order to describe the agencies that ...
   a have traveled to the moon.
   b have traveled to Mars.
   c want to travel to Mars.

4 The author mentions Sergei Krikalev to prove that ...
   a astronauts can spend a long time in space.
   b it is dangerous to send a human to Mars.
   c a human has already traveled to Mars.

5 According to the text, the author thinks that ...
   a governments should not spend money on space travel.
   b it is possible for humans to travel to Mars someday.
   c Mars is too cold for humans to survive there.

PART B ADDITIONAL SKILLS

2 Circle the correct answers.

1 Why do some people think it is easy to travel to the moon again?
  a Because it was easy to travel there in 1969.
  b Because robots often go to the moon.
  c Because today's technology is better than it was in the 1960s and 1970s.
2 What is the difference between manned and unmanned missions?
  a Manned missions are mission with people; unmanned missions are missions without people.
  b Manned missions go to the moon; unmanned missions go to planets.
  c NASA sends manned missions; ESA sends unmanned missions.
3 Why do NASA and ESA want to wait until the 2030s to send a manned mission to Mars?
  a Because Mars is too cold at the moment.
  b Because it is too far away.
  c Because it takes a long time to develop new technology.
4 How is Mars similar to the Earth?
  a The temperature is about the same as on Earth.
  b The atmosphere is nearly the same as on Earth.
  c Both planets have a lot of water.
5 Why does the writer say the journey to Mars would not be so bad?
  a Because it is safer than a journey to the moon.
  b Because one man has already spent more than twice as long in space.
  c Because the astronauts could sleep most of the time.

Name: _____   Date: _____

PART A KEY VOCABULARY

1 Circle the correct definitions for the words in bold.

1 As a child, I loved to **explore** the forest behind my house. There were so many interesting things to discover.
   a to stay away from a place because it looked strange
   b to go to a new place to learn about it

2 There are so many **advances** in movie technology that monsters and superheroes now appear to be real.
   a progress in the development or improvement of something
   b ways to make people believe something is true

3 People will not believe that aliens **exist** until they see them with their own eyes.
   a to look the same as humans
   b to be real, alive, or present

4 Antonio used to **wonder** what was at the bottom of the ocean, so he became an underwater photographer.
   a to study something in order to prove it is true
   b to think about something and try to understand it

5 The spacecraft **crashed** into the sea, but luckily there were no astronauts inside, and no one was hurt.
   a to hit something by accident, especially in a vehicle
   b to fail to reach the place you are trying to go

6 **Evidence** shows that the planet Venus has more than 1,600 volcanoes.
   a something that cannot be true
   b something that makes you believe something is true

7 **Entrepreneurs** like John Spencer, who founded the Space Tourism Society, believe that regular people will pay to travel in space someday.
   a people who start their own business
   b people who become CEOs at a young age

8 If a **private** space tourism company wants to go to Mars, they have to raise the money by themselves.
   a related to money or services controlled or supplied by a person or a company and not by the government
   b related to money or services controlled or supplied by the government and not by a person or company

2 Complete the sentences with the correct form of the words in the box.

beyond   condition   particular   prove   public   support   unlikely

1 In the past, governments usually sent people to space with _____ money. Today, more and more private companies, like SpaceX and Virgin Galactic, are interested in space tourism.

2 Traveling internationally is a good way to understand what is _____ the borders of your own country.

3 It is _____ that humans will travel to Jupiter in the near future because it is too far away.

4 Astronauts must exercise while they are in space in order to stay in good physical _____ .

5 Scientists are interested in all planets, but right now they have a(n) _____ interest in Mars.

6 Scientists think there may be another planet in our solar system. They named it Planet Nine and are doing research to _____ that it is exists.

7 Astronauts do experiments in space in order to _____ the work of scientists on Earth.

PART B LANGUAGE DEVELOPMENT
GIVING EVIDENCE AND SUPPORTING AN ARGUMENT

3 Choose the best word to complete each sentence.

1 *Experts / Reports* believe that our galaxy contains 200–400 million stars.
2 The latest research *thinks / shows* that most of space is made of "dark matter."
3 A recent report *suggests / believes* that an object called the Large Quasar Group (LQG) is the biggest thing in space.
4 *Research / Studies* suggest that humans may someday be able to farm on Mars.
5 Experts *think / show* that there is a very large black hole in the center of our galaxy.

Name: _____ Date: _____

PART A GRAMMAR FOR WRITING
THAT CLAUSES IN COMPLEX SENTENCES

1 Put the words in order to make complex sentences with *that* clauses.

1 it is too expensive / Some people / to travel in space / suggest that / .

_____

2 Doctors learned that / become weaker / astronauts' / muscles / in space / .

_____

3 the largest planet / are sure / that Jupiter is / Scientists / .

_____

4 it is difficult / Astronauts / know that / to sleep / well in space / .

_____

5 Pluto has / mountains as high as / Recent photos / 11,000 feet (3,353 meters) / show that / .

_____

INFINITIVES OF PURPOSE

2 Match the sentence halves.

1 She studies the stars _____
2 They sent a radio signal into space _____
3 We use satellites _____
4 I bought a new telescope _____
5 They take photos of the moon _____

a to study it more carefully.
b to help us understand the weather on Earth.
c to learn about what they are made of.
d to tell aliens how to find our planet.
e to see the stars more clearly.

PART B WRITING TASK

Should normal people travel to space?
Give reasons and examples to support your opinion.

3 Write an essay of three or four paragraphs. Include your opinion about the topic, support for your opinion, and a conclusion.

UNIT QUIZZES ANSWER KEY

UNIT 1 READING QUIZ
PART A KEY SKILLS

1 1 14 million 2 330 CE 3 1453 4 2.3 5 2016

PART B ADDITIONAL SKILLS

2 1 T
2 F; Istanbul is the biggest city in Turkey.
3 T
4 F; The Grand Bazaar is a market.
5 T
6 F; There are three bridges over the Bosporus.
7 F; The railway tunnel opened in 2013.
8 T

UNIT 1 LANGUAGE QUIZ
PART A KEY VOCABULARY

1 1 downtown 2 countryside 3 population
4 modern 5 local 6 traffic 7 cheap 8 area

2 1 b 2 b 3 a 4 b 5 a 6 a 7 b

PART B LANGUAGE DEVELOPMENT

3 1 adjective 2 adjective 3 verb 4 adjective
5 noun 6 adjective 7 adjective 8 noun
9 adjective 10 noun

4 1 expensives; expensive 2 beauty; beautiful
3 tradition; traditional 4 cities noisy; noisy cities
5 pollution; polluted

UNIT 1 WRITING QUIZ
PART A GRAMMAR FOR WRITING

1 1 My sister lives in a small town.
2 The city doesn't have a subway.
3 People shop in the downtown area.
4 The buildings are very tall.
5 Alex drives to work every day.

2 1 are 2 are 3 aren't 4 is 5 is

PART B WRITING TASK

3 *Answers will vary.*

UNIT 2 READING QUIZ
PART A KEY SKILLS

1 1 a 2 c 3 a, b, d, e

PART B ADDITIONAL SKILLS

2 1 T
2 F; People can see live snakes.
3 F; There is a five-mile footrace.
4 T
5 F; People throw tomatoes for one hour.
6 T
7 F; The cows travel from the mountains to the valleys.
8 T
9 T
10 T

UNIT 2 LANGUAGE QUIZ
PART A KEY VOCABULARY

1 1 celebrate 2 history 3 visitors 4 the ground
5 culture 6 highlight

2 1 e 2 d 3 c 4 a 5 f 6 b

PART B LANGUAGE DEVELOPMENT

3 1 in 2 on 3 in 4 on 5 at 6 In 7 In 8 In
9 At 10 at 11 at

4 1 We **always** go to Rio de Janeiro for Carnival.
2 I **usually** spend my birthday with my family.
3 The Chinese New Year **sometimes** starts in January. / **Sometimes** the Chinese New Year starts in January. / The Chinese New Year starts in January **sometimes**.
4 We **never** go to parties.
5 At the festival, people **often** exchange gifts with friends and relatives.

UNIT 2 WRITING QUIZ
PART A GRAMMAR FOR WRITING

1 1 We eat traditional food.
2 My mother wears a new dress.
3 The music starts at midnight.
4 I give my sister a gift.
5 My family celebrates for three days.

2 1 People celebrate the festival of Diwali in India.
2 Everyone wears new clothes on the third day.
3 People light small lanterns in their houses.
4 They draw flowers on the ground.
5 People give gifts to their loved ones.

PART B WRITING TASK

3 *Answers will vary.*

UNIT 3 READING QUIZ
PART A KEY SKILLS

1 1 a 2 b 3 b 4 a 5 a

2 1 c 2 c 3 b 4 c 5 a

UNIT 3 LANGUAGE QUIZ
PART A KEY VOCABULARY

1 1 free 2 affect 3 interest 4 educational
5 software 6 security 7 collect

2 1 a 2 b 3 a 4 b 5 b 6 a 7 a

PART B LANGUAGE DEVELOPMENT

3 1 video game / computer game 2 email address /
Web address 3 smartphone 4 keyboard
5 computer program 6 Web page

4 1 I think that online shopping is usually safe.
2 It seems to me that social media is very popular.
3 In my opinion, some video games aren't suitable for
children.
4 I think (that) the Internet has made life easier.
5 I believe (that) Internet banking is better than
traditional banking.

UNIT 3 WRITING QUIZ
PART A GRAMMAR FOR WRITING

1 1 I have an email account, but I don't use it now.
2 I use the Internet, and I have two email accounts.
3 My friends shop online a lot, but I like shopping at
regular stores.
4 Some video games are fun to play, and they can
teach children about math.
5 Social media is very popular, but it hasn't replaced
traditional media.

2 1 I buy films online. I also upload my own films.
2 You can read news articles on this website. You can
read people's comments, too.
3 The Internet has many advantages. However, it also
has some disadvantages.
4 I have a bank account online. I shop online a lot,
too.
5 I buy books on the Internet. You can also buy
videos on the Internet.

PART B WRITING TASK

3 *Answers will vary.*

UNIT 4 READING QUIZ
PART A KEY SKILLS

1 2, 3, 4, 8, 9

2 1 balloons 2 cows 3 better 4 east
5 wet grass

PART B ADDITIONAL SKILLS

3 1 c 2 b 3 a 4 a 5 b

UNIT 4 LANGUAGE QUIZ
PART A KEY VOCABULARY

1 1 c 2 d 3 e 4 a 5 g 6 b 7 f

2 1 precipitation 2 careful 3 rise 4 shock
5 dangerous 6 thunder

PART B LANGUAGE DEVELOPMENT

3 1 high 2 low 3 rises 4 increase 5 reaches
6 maximum 7 falls 8 decrease 9 minimum
10 drops

UNIT 4 WRITING QUIZ
PART A GRAMMAR FOR WRITING

1 1 hottest 2 higher 3 sunnier 4 most dangerous
5 lowest 6 drier 7 rainiest 8 more extreme
9 biggest 10 easier

PART B WRITING TASK

2 *Answers will vary.*

UNIT 5 READING QUIZ
PART A KEY SKILLS

1 1 T 2 T 3 F 4 T 5 F

PART B ADDITIONAL SKILLS

2 1 c 2 a 3 a 4 c 5 b

UNIT 5 LANGUAGE QUIZ
PART A KEY VOCABULARY

1 1 ancient 2 take place 3 challenging 4 in shape
5 Swimming 6 course 7 accident

2 1 b 2 b 3 a 4 b 5 a 6 a

PART B LANGUAGE DEVELOPMENT

3 1 across 2 past 3 through 4 around 5 over

UNIT 5 WRITING QUIZ
PART A GRAMMAR FOR WRITING

1 1 brother 2 throws 3 watch 4 players 4 runs

2 1 need 2 catch 3 are 4 watches 5 try

PART B WRITING TASK

3 *Answers will vary.*

UNIT 6 READING QUIZ
PART A KEY SKILLS

1 1 a 2 b 3 a 4 b 5 a

2 1 c 2 c 3 a 4 a 5 a

PART B ADDITIONAL SKILLS

3 1 F; The Tata Group helps a lot of people.
  2 T
  3 F; The most expensive company was Corus.
  4 F; The Nano is the world's cheapest car.
  5 T

UNIT 6 LANGUAGE QUIZ
PART A KEY VOCABULARY

1 1 results 2 occupation 3 advertise 4 run
  5 colleagues 6 partner 7 customers

2 1 e 2 a 3 g 4 f 5 c 6 d 7 b

PART B LANGUAGE DEVELOPMENT

3 1 expand 2 plan 3 set up 4 partner
  5 contact

4 1 I share my office with two other people.
  2 The new software helped my computer run better.
  3 The employee asked his boss for a day off.
  4 A new product must be tested for quality.
  5 The mall employs more than 500 people.

UNIT 6 WRITING QUIZ
PART A GRAMMAR FOR WRITING

1 1 makes 2 employs 3 started 4 made
  5 produced 6 sold 7 was 8 started
  9 works 10 are

2 1 When the partners had enough money, they set up their business. / The partners set up their business when they had enough money.
  2 When the employee quit his job, he found a job that paid more money.
  3 When the company's product failed, they introduced a new product.
  4 When the economy improved, the business made more money. / The business made more money when the economy improved.
  5 When cell phones were invented, people could communicate more easily. / People could communicate more easily when cell phones were invented.

PART B WRITING TASK

3 *Answers will vary.*

UNIT 7 READING QUIZ
PART A KEY SKILLS

1 1 No; paragraph 2, sentence 2–3 2 Yes; paragraph 3, sentences 3–5 3 No; paragraph 4, sentence 2
  4 Yes; paragraph 4, sentence 4 5 Yes; paragraph 5, sentences 3–4

PART B ADDITIONAL SKILLS

2 1 b 2 c 3 a 4 c 5 c

UNIT 7 LANGUAGE QUIZ
PART A KEY VOCABULARY

1 1 a 2 b 3 a 4 a 5 b 6 b 7 a

2 1 operation 2 take care of 3 inspired 4 former
  5 train 6 dream 7 honest

PART B LANGUAGE DEVELOPMENT

3 1 at the end of the film 2 a kind /a type of computer 3 at the top of the building 4 a kind / a type of music 5 the manager of the IT department

4 1 patient 2 selfish 3 kind 4 intelligent
  5 difficult

UNIT 7 WRITING QUIZ
PART A GRAMMAR FOR WRITING

1 1 Role models *should/must/have to* be reliable.
2 Role models *should not/must not* be difficult.
3 Role models *should/must/have to* respect other people's opinions.
4 Role models *should not/must not* be lazy.
5 Role models *should/must/have to* be kind.

PART B WRITING TASK

2 *Answers will vary.*

UNIT 8 READING QUIZ
PART A KEY SKILLS

1 1 c 2 b 3 c 4 a 5 b

PART B ADDITIONAL SKILLS

2 1 c 2 a 3 c 4 c 5 b

UNIT 8 LANGUAGE QUIZ
PART A KEY VOCABULARY

1 1 b 2 a 3 b 4 b 5 a 6 b 7 a 8 a

2 1 public 2 beyond 3 unlikely 4 condition
5 particular 6 prove 7 support

PART B LANGUAGE DEVELOPMENT

3 1 Experts 2 shows 3 suggests 4 Studies
5 think

UNIT 8 WRITING QUIZ
PART A GRAMMAR FOR WRITING

1 1 Some people suggest that it is too expensive to travel in space.
2 Doctors learned that astronauts' muscles become weaker in space.
3 Scientists are sure that Jupiter is the largest planet.
4 Astronauts know that it is difficult to sleep well in space.
5 Recent photos show that Pluto has mountains as high as 11,000 feet (3,353 meters).

2 1 c 2 d 3 b 4 e 5 a

PART B WRITING TASK

3 *Answers will vary.*

CREDITS

The authors and publishers acknowledge the following sources of copyright material and are grateful for the permissions granted. While every effort has been made, it has not always been possible to identify the sources of all the material used, or to trace all copyright holders. If any omissions are brought to our notice, we will be happy to include the appropriate acknowledgements on reprinting and in the next update to the digital edition, as applicable.

Photo credits

p. 45 (photo 1): Jared Hobbs/All Canada Photos/Getty Images; p. 45 (photo 2): Anadolu Agency/Getty Images; p. 45 (photo 3): filmfoto/ iStock Editorial/Getty Images Plus/Getty Images; p. 45 (photo 4): Atid Kiattisaksiri/LightRocket/Getty Images;

Front cover photographs by (man) SharpPhoto/Shutterstock and (BG) PlusONE/Shutterstock.

Illustrations

by Integra p. 63.

Corpus

Development of this publication has made use of the Cambridge English Corpus (CEC). The CEC is a multi-billion word computer database of contemporary spoken and written English. It includes British English, American English, and other varieties of English. It also includes the Cambridge Learner Corpus, developed in collaboration with the University of Cambridge ESOL Examinations. Cambridge University Press has built up the CEC to provide evidence about language use that helps to produce better language teaching materials

Cambridge Dictionaries

Cambridge dictionaries are the world's most widely used dictionaries for learners of English. The dictionaries are available in print and online at dictionary.cambridge.org. Copyright © Cambridge University Press, reproduced with permission.

Typeset by emc design ltd